Refle

Also by Ron Scolastico, Ph.D.

THE EARTH ADVENTURE:
Your Soul's Journey Through Physical Reality

HEALING THE HEART, HEALING THE BODY:
*A Spiritual Perspective on
Emotional, Mental, and Physical Health*

Reflections

Inspired Wisdom On:

Gods and Symbols	*Education*
The Human Mind	*Healing Addictions*
Angels and Guides	*Healing the Hurt Child*

Ron Scolastico, Ph.D.

Hay House, Inc.
Carson, California

REFLECTIONS
by Ron Scolastico, Ph.D.

Copyright © 1993 by Ron Scolastico

Library of Congress Cataloging-in-Publication Data

Scolastico, Ronald B. (Ronald Barry)
    Reflections : inspired wisdom on Gods and symbols, the human mind, angels and guides, education, healing addictions, healing the hurt child / Ron Scolastico.
        p.   cm.
    ISBN 1-56170-065-7 (pbk.) : $12.95
      1. Spiritual life—Miscellanea. 2. God—Miscellanea.
  3. Symbolism—Miscellanea. 4. Intellect—Miscellanea.
  5. Eduation—Miscellanea. 6. Psychology, Pathological—
Miscellanea.   I. Title
BL624.S385   1993
133—dc20   93–17056
                                                    CIP

Library of Congress Catalog Card No. 93–17056
ISBN: 1-56170-065-7

93 94 95 96 97 98   10 9 8 7 6 5 4 3 2 1
First Printing, August 1993

Published and Distributed in the United States by:

Hay House, Inc.
P.O. Box 6204
Carson, CA 90749-6204

Printed in the United States of America on Recycled Paper

After close on two centuries of passionate struggles, neither science nor faith has succeeded in discrediting its adversary. On the contrary, it becomes obvious that neither can develop normally without the other. And the reason is simple: the same life animates both. Neither in its impetus nor its achievement can science go to its limits without becoming tinged with mysticism and charged with faith.

Pierre Teilhard de Chardin

*This book is dedicated to
my wife, Susan Scolastico,
with great gratitude for
her inspiration, wisdom, and love,
and to those who are seeking
a deeper experience of
the spiritual realities
that sustain our life on earth.*

Contents

Publisher's Note

This book presents reflections of a larger reality than the one we usually experience in our day to day lives. It has been written by a distinguished transpersonal psychologist who has explored that larger reality thousands of times.

Ron Scolastico has developed a unique ability to enter a deep state of consciousness and draw upon a vast source of wisdom that lies outside of our ordinary awareness. From that state of expanded consciousness, Dr. Scolastico speaks in depth on many subjects. This profound knowledge is recorded on audio tape and then transcribed. The books that he creates through this process offer valuable insights into human psychological patterns, as well as a brilliant vision of the spiritual realities that underlie human existence.

Dr. Scolastico learned to access this vast source of wisdom in 1978. (He describes his process of discovery of this source in his book, *The Earth Adventure: Your Soul's Journey Through Physical Reality*, published by Hay House.) Since 1978, he has drawn upon this source more than 14,000 times to provide inspired counseling and teaching sessions for individuals and groups throughout the world. He has also attuned to this source to create numerous audio tapes and books that offer insights into many important aspects of our existence—from specific personal issues of daily life, through broad philosophical and metaphysical questions, to an understanding of modern society and the place of humanity in the unfoldment of life on earth.

In discussing the source of the wisdom to which he attunes, Dr. Scolastico has said:

> "I believe that I am drawing upon knowledge that is potentially available to everyone. We have many different ideas and concepts about the *source* of this knowledge. Psychologists may call it *the collective unconscious*, or *race memory*. Some people prefer vague terms, such as *intuitive wisdom*, or simply, *inspiration*. Others might think in terms of *spiritual guides*, or *guardian angels*. Since we cannot yet objectively verify the non-physical source of knowledge that is available to us, I encourage each person to use whatever concept or explanation seems true to him or her.
>
> "In my own work with this source of knowledge, I am not so concerned with defining it. The important thing to me is whether the information that comes forth is helpful to people in their day to day lives."

This book, *Reflections*, presents inspired wisdom brought forth by Dr. Scolastico in six different subject areas. They are: (1) Gods and Symbols, (2) The Human Mind, (3) Angels and Guides, (4) Education, (5) Healing Addictions, and, (6) Healing the Hurt Child. Each of these subjects is addressed in its own chapter. Every chapter begins with an opening teaching that explores the psychological and spiritual aspects of the subject. This is followed by answers given to specific questions asked in the subject area. Each chapter concludes with an uplifting closing summary.

When Dr. Scolastico speaks from his inspired state of consciousness, the language is a bit different than current usage. In order to make this language more understandable and easier to read, Dr. Scolastico has edited the transcripts of the following chapters. However, the unique flavor or the language has been left intact in order to capture the loving and inspiring feeling of the source of knowledge as it expresses through Dr. Scolastico.

Reflections

Chapter One

GODS AND SYMBOLS

Perceiving Spiritual Realities

As we come forth with you now to help you understand the way that your human mind and emotions will draw forth knowledge to yourself concerning the forces of the spiritual life, and the way that knowledge is introduced into your mind—which is often through a rather symbolic kind of representation—in order to adjust for the tendency in the human mind to distort toward personal preference and personal desire, we would gently suggest that in this period while you would work with us, you would try, as best you can, to pretend that you are not yourself. Pretend that you are not the human being who has many desires to have certain fulfillments, whose life must go in a certain direction to please you, who would feel a great fear of certain challenges—all of which causes in you a prejudice toward certain ways of believing about life, and seeing life. Those influences also cause within you a certain "repulsion" to other ways of seeing life that might be negative, or challenging to your personality.

So, in a gentle way, imagine that in this moment you are putting aside your, so to speak, "baggage" of human personality preference and dislike, which ordinarily you must work with in each day. Put that aside as we speak of broad areas of truth that affect the entire human race, that affect human beings who have a different vision of life than you do—which includes your friends, as well as your enemies, and includes living human beings, and those who have made death. If you would try to understand the areas that we will speak of filtered through your prejudices, you might gain a bit of knowledge, but you would tend to warp the truths in the direction of your own beliefs and prejudices. So, make a gentle imagination that your beliefs, your cares, your worries, your desires, and all that makes up your own personal life, which is so important to you ordinarily, for this period of working with us, imagine that these are gently set aside.

Try to feel now that you are much larger than your ordinary human self. Feel a new sense of belonging to the entire human race. Feel that you are connected to all human beings. And let those kinds of feelings permeate you as we enter now into a deeper understanding of what it is that makes up the forces of creativity that feed you— the energies that you would call the forces of God.

Let us begin with a certain vision of the past. In the past, most of you present human beings were a part of the incoming waves of the first human habitation of earth. In terms of the human counting of time, this habitation would be extremely ancient.

To simplify and abbreviate a complex process that led up to the first habitation, we would say that those first waves of human expression were initiated by eternal souls, who were created by forces of God. Those eternal souls decided to make an expression of themselves that would be unique in all realities. Their expression first initiated the creation of space. Then it resulted in the creation of time. Then, over eons of that time, the souls' expression brought about the creation of the hard matter in space, including all of the universes, stars, and so forth. Then, there comes the earth itself, and the physical evolution of the earth, guided by the overwatching souls.

In very ancient periods, those souls would project a portion of themselves into a kind of body that, at first, would *not* be physical. You would consider these bodies to be "energy" forms.

Gradually, the energy patterns within the non-physical human bodies would be "imposed" upon certain evolving animal forms, so that in time, you would have the appearance of the present human body as you know it.

The portion of a soul that was projected into one human body could be called the *human personality matrix*. Within you now is such a personality matrix of energies from your own soul. Those energies enable you to be aware of yourself as a human being—to be aware of your thoughts, your feelings, your ideas, your memories, your longings, and all of your other inner experiences. Your personality matrix also includes eternal forces from your soul that animate you and stimulate you.

All of those energies, woven into a personality matrix, entering a physical body at birth, create what you consider to be the present human experience. However, when you walked in those ancient periods inside a physical human body as a personality matrix, your inner experience was quite different. It is difficult to put the difference in words. We shall attempt to do so.

In the present, as a modern human being, you are concerned with, first of all, your well being—whether you have enough to eat, a place to live, ones to love you, work to do, money to master the physical world, things such as that. And, from your point of view, the most striking aspect of reality is that it is *solid* and *physical*. In your present human experience, this physical world takes most of your time and attention.

However, in the early stages of the human race, you ones had very little interest in the physical world. You needed to eat, and rest, and move about in your physical bodies, but, in those beginning portions, the personality matrix was so steeped in a direct perception of *eternal forces*, of *the life of the souls* that animated you ones as humans, of *the forces of God*, that you had very little difficulty simply "looking" and directly "seeing" God.

Now, when we use the rather limited human words, "looking and seeing God," you must translate them into a different understanding than what you ordinarily associate with such words. In those ancient times, you did not look with your physical eyes and see God as a human figure standing before you. You looked with your heart, with abilities that you would now call *emotion* and *intuition*. And, even from inside your physical human body, you did feel the extraordinary forces of this God—forces which can only be described in human words, quite inadequately, as *love*, *creativity*, *wisdom*, *sensitivity*, *comfort*, *joy*, and so forth. So, rather than physically seeing God, you would actually *experience* God.

Thus, in the early portions of human life, you did not need to *think* of God. You did not need to translate God into a symbolic representation for your five physical senses. You did not need to see God, or hear God, or taste God, or touch God, or smell God—all of those physical responses. You knew of God inwardly as your being. Inside your human awareness, you lived primarily in a world that would be considered to be *spiritual*.

At that time, the physical life on earth was simply interesting. It is as though you are busily engaged in a wonderful love affair that is very joyful and all consuming, and you decide to go to the theater. The play is interesting, but you do not feel, "This is the most important event in my life." It is simply interesting. You feel that the love affair is the most important event in your life. So, in a sense, to put it simply, in those early periods, you would have a love affair with God, with your souls, and with the eternal realities from which you spring, and in which your own soul—which is still you—has its continuing existence. You would be fascinated by the earth life, and interested in it, as though it were an amusing addition—a small one—to your expression as a projection of an eternal soul.

In such an existence, there was little use for symbols. And, in a certain way of speaking, the human intelligence was not yet evolved enough to make much sense out of symbols or intellectual creations and subtleties. There would simply be a quite wonderful experience, intended by the souls for the human personalities, and it would move in harmonious and extremely perfect ways, according to the patterns of intentions of the souls, and the intentions of the forces that you would call God.

Now, as the evolution of these beginning human experiences would come about, the souls would desire, through their human personalities, a more intense experience of human life. Let us say, to extend our analogy, that your love affair is so intense that you cannot enjoy the theater. You would say, "I wish to enjoy this play a bit more intensely. I will take some time away from my love affair. I will ask my beloved one to give me the freedom to go watch plays for a longer period of time, for I wish more intensity in my experience of those plays." In a way, this provides a crude example of why the eternal souls would begin a process of gradually disengaging the human awareness from its full intuitive perceptions of eternal truths and eternal forces. To simplify many complex areas, we would say that, over a long period of time, human generations came to feel that they actually live in the temporary theater of physical reality, rather than in the love affair with their eternal existence.

This change in human awareness was not an error, nor a flaw. It was an intention of the souls, knowing that they could launch a long evolutionary process in which human beings would take earth life seriously, and commit themselves to earth life. The souls, all the while, knew that they are eternal, and that there is no loss caused by the human personality temporarily putting aside the spiritual perceptions.

Thus, over long periods of time—and now we are simplifying many things—there would eventually come about a human existence relatively like your present one, in which your physical sensory perceptions dominate your life. What you see, hear, touch, taste, and smell becomes reality for you.

As this change in human awareness occurred, of course, there was still a longing in human beings to know the truth of God and the eternal realities. In the early stages of the concretizing, or solidifying of the human life into physical matter, there would be some human beings that you would call priests, or holy ones, who would feel that there must be continual reminders of the spiritual realms. Thus, they would dedicate their lives to *not* enmeshing themselves in the new preoccupation with physical life on earth. Rather, they would focus upon attaining deep spiritual experiences, and they would, at times, teach other ones of their deeper experiences. In essence, they would initiate traditions of a spiritual and mystical nature—verbal at first, then later recorded in written language—that would keep alive the knowledge of the eternal realms, and feed it into humanity. We are simplifying many thousands of years of human experience in all of this.

Next, the *intelligence* of the human race would receive attention from the eternal souls. The eternal souls would sharpen their creative capacities and begin to stimulate human intelligence—the human mind. As human beings began to think more and more, the souls intended for them to continue *feeling* deeply. But, for many reasons—primarily self indulgence, selfishness, preoccupation with personal desires, using the mind in the service of desires that would tend to be selfish, and the creation of human fear, mistrust, misunderstanding, and other negativity— through the ages, there has gradually come about a rather strong over-emphasis upon the intellectual capacities of human beings. You ones have still continued to evolve your feeling capacity, but, in the modern time in particular, for many ones, the intellect rules, so to speak, over emotion. Of course, there are many who do not manifest this general pattern.

As the intellectual creativity and activity have grown, and as the hunger to know God has been kept alive in human beings by the souls, there has come about the *intellectual* pursuit of God and truth, which at times, overshadows the *feeling* of God. Gradually, most ones in the modern time have temporarily lost that deep capacity to directly perceive God through intuition and inner feeling. They now rely upon *thinking* about God, and *studying* God. Such activities from past times have brought about the fascination with symbolic representations of God, of truth, and of life.

This is a beginning understanding to help you place your mind in a broader context.

QUESTION: Because there are so many differing ideas about God, would you discuss what God is, from your perspective?

As we look at this with you, we would ask that you hold in your mind this possibility: "Perhaps one of my purposes in this lifetime, in addition to the fulfillment of all of the human desires that are important to me, is to create my own unique, individual understanding of, and perception of God."

In the past, when humans were tending to group together in herds, like sheep, and the intelligence of human beings was low, not yet fully evolved, human beings needed crude, simple, shared ideas, perceptions, and thoughts. So, when the human beings lost their capacity to directly perceive what is God through their own feeling, intuition, and inner sensitivity, they began to create shared *ideas* and *beliefs*, and even *symbolic visions* of God, that enabled them all to help one another "hang on" to God, so to speak.

Many times these shared visions of God would revolve about the experience of one individual who had learned to inwardly perceive God, somewhat, and the group then would share that individual's perception. Often, they would build a teaching, or religion upon that individual's perception of God.

This is an old pattern that served humanity well for many ages. But, in this present period, given the high intelligence of human beings, and given all of the knowledge that you ones have accumulated intellectually, and shared with one another throughout this earth, there is such a potent expression of human individuality—the uniqueness of the individual human being—that there are not many conceptions and ideas of God that can now fully serve large numbers of people. Thus, you might take a conception as your starting point for your understanding of God, but, we gently suggest that you consider that it is your responsibility to create your own private understanding of God. You can draw upon the teachings and experiences of others, if it pleases you, but that is only a starting point.

If one says to you, "God is a large horse, standing at the edge of the world, turning a motor with a wheel by walking on a large stone that is circular," you would find this rather amusing. Your mind has gone far beyond such crude symbols. But, in the past, in a certain Polynesian experience, that image would have excited you.

At the present time, the important question is not, What is God? It is: *What stimulates your personal experience and understanding of God?* As an individual human being, only *you* could say what does that to the largest extent. So, when we try to convey to you in words what God is, we must focus upon your individual capacity to think God, to feel God, to imagine God, to create God.

Your work to do this must be built upon an assumption that there *is* a God, but that your ability to directly perceive God has been blocked by your over-focus upon intellect and physical reality. You can make some adjustments mentally and emotionally, learning to take periods of silence, calmness, and patience each day, quieting your ordinary human thoughts and feelings, and gradually you can reactivate your intuitive capacity to feel God.

However, what you feel God as, or how you feel it, will be determined by your *beliefs*. If you are satisfied that God is a large horse, and you take periods of silence to focus upon that, after a while, you can perceive God as a large horse. One could not say, "God is *not* a large horse," since the forces of life and God live in all large horses. But, God is much more than a large horse. You can see the individual nature of perception here.

God is not an object that we are trying to help you delineate. It is not a box lying on a table that we could describe for you precisely. It is an extraordinary kind of reality, and the only words that you have for that reality are "force," or "energy." But, those words are so empty, compared to the extraordinary lovingness of the forces of God.

So, we could say, as a suggestion to you, if you are one who responds to broad concepts, begin with the concept that God is the most extraordinary force, most unendingly loving reality, that has created you and all of life. And, that extraordinary force, or reality, has a personal relationship to you, and to your eternal soul.

This you could take as a very general beginning, and then build upon it with whatever touches your heart. If you already have strong ideas of God, and if they move you toward *love*, then use them. If your strong ideas of God move you toward *criticism* of yourself and others, then we suggest that they are a distortion created by your human personality, for the forces of God would never move you toward negativity. Thus, if your ideas and feelings about God would say, "God will punish me for this if I am bad," we assure you that this is not a perception of God. It is a human distortion.

Learning to perceive God is a lifetime activity that needs to be woven with your lifetime of pursuing your own individual goals and fulfillments. The more successful you are at working to feel God, understand God, and live God, the more successful will be your human life on earth. If you ignore God totally, you can have some fulfillments, you can complete some purposes, but that extraordinary depth of completion that you hunger for will be difficult to achieve.

At this time, we cannot describe God for you in human words. We can only assure you that God is a reality, much more real than your present physical body, your present human life, and your present physical earth and the universe around it. God is much more real than your limited ideas about life. Yet, you have the power to create a *feeling* that seems true to you that says, "There is no God. There is only emptiness beyond human life." You have the freedom to do that. You also have the freedom to suffer from that limited perception.

We strongly suggest that, whatever you do to perceive God, always be aware that your perceptions will be smaller than God. By your human nature, you are temporarily squeezed into small abilities of perception. You will need to work diligently throughout this lifetime to expand your perceptions. Begin with your feelings. The more you can feel the love that is God, then the more your mind will be guided into a more brilliant and creative use of symbols and ideas to represent God. But, know in your heart that if you only think about God and represent God symbolically, even though that benefits you, it does not bring the depth of completion that *feeling* God can bring.

QUESTION: Would you trace the evolution of our spiritual nature, or consciousness, from the point where the physical, sensory awareness became more of our reality? How have we evolved in our understanding of God over time, and where are we headed with our understanding?

First of all, your focus upon physical matter and the intellect was *intended* by the souls. So, you would see it as an expression of God. The forces of God do live inside you, whether you feel them or not. They live in you as your thoughts about physical reality. Even thoughts that you might call "evil," are enabled to happen because of forces of God. The thoughts are turned toward negativity because of human *fear* and *misunderstanding*. Therefore, regardless of human negativity, the evolution of the intellect, along with all of the other human expressions, is an expression of God.

When you try to look back upon, or reflect upon what lives inside you that enables you to live, and to be aware of yourself, you are engaging in an activity that flows counter to the stream of physical evolution. In other words, human beings have embarked upon an intellectual, physical mastery of the world. This mastery is an expression of the souls, and the souls are an expression of God. However, in accomplishing this mastery, human beings were not intended to ignore their finer perceptions of God. They were intended to weave those perceptions with the intellectual and physical mastery of the world. But, as humans have moved from the past to the present modern times, in general, the evolution of human spiritual perceptions has involved a kind of unintended numbing, and dulling of the finer perceptions. Many human beings have lost interest in weaving the finer intuitive perceptions of the spiritual world into their day to day life. Although some have kept alive the religious, spiritual traditions, others have ignored them.

In general, speaking crudely, we would say that the human evolution of spiritual perception has been diminished because of *human choices*, and not as a consequence of pursuing your task of subduing and mastering the physical world. You could master the physical world, and at the same time you could open your perceptions of the spiritual world. The intended evolution was to lead you to do both at the same time. But, because of human distortion, many ones are doing only the first—the physical mastery. This is not bad nor wrong. It is simply less fulfilling for you.

Gradually, many, particularly in the modern period, are beginning to realize that the physical world by itself is not enough. Eating, drinking, sleeping, having sexual union and love affairs, accumulating money, and other physical fulfillments, although they are all part of the physical mastery, and they bring some joy, they are not enough. They do not give you a deep enough experience of *meaning* in life. They are not enough *purpose* in life.

Some of you have opened the door to finer perceptions through *love*. Often, if you dedicate yourself to the loving of other human beings, it is much more than the other limited fulfillments. But, even that is not enough. If you do not understand that you are eternal, then loving other human beings is not fully satisfying when you are facing death, or when there is much pain and suffering in human life.

Gradually, many of you have stirred up an underlying hunger to know the spiritual truth of life—to know God. Some of you have totally turned away from the physical in confusion, believing that it is the cause of the challenge. Others have realized: "My perception of God is evolving individually. And, it is time for the human race to evolve their perception of God. But, this does not mean that we deny the mastery of the physical. For that is a part of the purposes we have been working so diligently toward, for ages and ages."

In the future, the evolution of the human capacity to perceive spiritually, most likely—if you ones respond to the impulses of guidance being given by your souls—would include a continued celebration of the mastery of the physical world, and a rejoicing in it, but with more love for other human beings. And, gradually, you will gain a clearer and clearer perception of the forces of God that live in human life, until you regain those intended, clear, direct perceptions of God. Then, you will see God everywhere, in all of the physical life, in all of the physical world. You will see God as *not* separate from you, not separate from your mastery of the physical world, not separate from anything. That is the kind of human experience that you are evolving toward.

QUESTION: Speaking of the time when humanity worshipped many gods, is there something in the actual hierarchy of spiritual realities that would have prompted the worship of such mythological gods as Thor, Zeus, and so forth?

As we look with you now to those stages of the human lives, and the human understandings and perceptions of that time, we will generalize some common threads, although these would vary among individuals.

First of all, in the early stages of worship of what you now call mythological gods, there would be those who had lost their capacity to directly perceive God through inner feelings, and who were developing a growing fascination with the intellectual life. In the first generations of humans who would create the worship of mythological gods—not the later generations who would take the gods as *teachings* and follow them by rote—there would be in certain societies, particularly in societies around the Mediterranean area, some human beings who had kept alive the passion for knowing: "What is the purpose of life? What created us as human beings? What animates us and keeps us alive?"

These ones would generally be in families. In other words, the elder members of a family would engage in this kind of introspection by temporarily disengaging from the physical world. They would either go into the mountains, the deserts, or the caves. They were intuitively prompted to do this, not taught by tradition.

Since their inner perceptions were blocked, they could not see God inwardly, but, in a way, they would *feel* God as something extraordinarily large. It is as though you have come into a foggy valley. There is something very large in front of you. Let us say that you have just been to the zoo on the previous day. Then, you would say, "There is an elephant." However, it might be a mountain. It might be a house. You cannot see clearly, so your *interpretation* is that it is an elephant. This a crude way to say that early human beings would attribute *forms* to the forces of God, and those forms came out of their feelings and their imagination.

Also, in some portions of earlier human expression, before the ordinary human bodies were solidified, there were certain "experiments" carried out by the souls over eons of time. This was done in the period when the bodies were more plastic and malleable. The souls would often, let us say, in human terms, "amuse themselves," by the creation of rather unusual forms. Some were extremely large, some were animal in nature, and some had human kinds of expressions. These were very ancient experiments, and they were gradually dissolved and eliminated. But, there was another stream of ordinary humans who would keep alive the *tales* of those ancient creatures.

So, there would be two streams of input to the beliefs in mythological gods. One was the inward perceptions of those sensitive human beings, usually the elders, who would dedicate themselves to inward pursuits, and would translate their feelings of God, which were very foggy and crude, into their own imaginary forms. The other stream would be the tales of unusual creatures that were kept alive, and which would then become gods in the retelling of the tales.

QUESTION: Human psychology has taught us certain things about symbols and symbolism. From a spiritual perspective, are there deeper understandings that you can give us about symbols and the way they affect our lives as human beings?

You can consider that, essentially, your symbolic creations are *human*. They are an expression of a growing intelligence in the human race. The more complex your intelligence becomes, and the more your ability to think complex things grows, the more complex your symbols will become. When you enter into areas that have no human equivalents—they are not solid matter—such as spiritual guides, forces of God, memories of past times of earth which live only unconsciously in most ones, and many other different realities that have no human forms, then the human passion for explaining, studying, and understanding—which is part of your mastery of earth life—prompts you to create *forms* for the unknown. Those forms become your symbols.

We could say that there are two broad categories of symbols created by human beings that represent all that is unknown. The first category would be the symbols that represent unknowns in the *eternal* realities that are not physical. These realities include God, souls, guiding ones, and many beings beyond your present understanding.

You ones have also created symbols to represent the unknowns of *human* life. What is that unknown motivating impulse that causes one human being to strike out at another? What is that impulse that causes a human being to intuitively love, even though there is not a developed relationship with another? What are those hidden impulses that you ascribe to the unconscious mind? There are many mysterious unconscious forces and energies that you cannot perceive, and you assume they have something to do with your thinking, feeling, and behavior as human beings. And, often, you ones, particularly psychologists who are fascinated with the unknown, will create interesting symbols for those unconscious areas.

Since you lack *direct perception* of the invisible, you could say that symbols are better than nothing. At least symbols give you something to think about, study, move around, and try to do something with. But, in terms of human evolution, symbols are as though a child is scribbling simple letters on a board, compared to a scientist writing calculus equations on the board. At the present stage, your understanding of symbols is quite immature. But, this is not to say that it is *wrong*. If the child does not learn to scribble simple letters, it will not learn to write words, and do mathematics. So, paying attention to symbolic representations of invisible things—eternal things, and invisible energies and forces that live in the human personality—is a very important part of your life.

The actual *use* of symbols, of course, is dominated by your personality. It is dominated by your motives in using symbols. You might say, "I wish to use symbols to become more loving and kind." Another person might use the same set of symbols, saying, "I wish to manipulate people to fulfill my desires." You will not find the power of *result* in the symbols themselves, but in the way that human beings use them. In a sense, symbols are *mirrors*. They show more about you as the user of them, than they do about the symbols and what those symbols represent to human beings.

To illustrate this, let us say that you are one who symbolizes God as an elderly male human being sitting upon a throne. In the traditional Christian beliefs, there are many who are drawn to this symbol. Now, one Christian, if we can use that grouping, would see in that male human being sitting on a throne, a great kindness and gentleness, and would say, "God is love." Another Christian, in the same symbol, would see a desire to punish human beings for their sins, and would say, "God is power." Each of you will need to be familiar with your own personality, your own habits of thinking and feeling, your own prejudices, your likes, your desires, your various beliefs, and all of those areas, so that you are clearly aware of what you bring to symbols.

What human beings have brought to symbols through the ages, of course, has wildly fluctuated. In times of struggle, famine, and horrible events, human beings, in general, have brought quite *negative* interpretations to religious and other symbols. In times of harmony and peace, there is a tendency to bring more loving interpretations to symbols.

There are some patterns in physical reality that you might call "geometric patterns," symbolically speaking. In other words, there are certain ways that the eternal forces *organize* reality, for which there are no human words. There are no words to describe those soul actions. To attempt to translate them into something that you can understand, we could say that the energies of God—and this is not literal, but a symbol to represent what has no words—the forces of God could be spoken of as having certain "shapes" and "forms." You could understand them as geometric shapes, although you would not look out into spiritual realms and see squares and triangles floating around in space. There are organizations to those forces. So, let us call them geometric forces.

Geometric forces, when perceived and internalized by human beings as symbolic shapes, for example, in nature, as the triangle of a mountain, or the circle of a pond, and so forth, trigger an unconscious sensitivity to the eternal forces of God and souls that have their own forms—forms that you cannot perceive. Gradually, over the ages, human beings have associated certain shapes and forms with the underlying energies of God that created those forms. Those physical shapes and forms are not the energies of God, but they feel like them. This has led human beings through the ages to identify some of those deeper feelings about shapes and forms with certain physical objects.

In a crude way of speaking, let us say that human beings associate a sinuosity, or a slipperiness, or a sliminess, to a snake. And, some of the forces of God have to do with malleability, flexibility, slipperiness, and sinuosity. In a way, human beings internalize and develop certain inner feelings about snakes. Those feelings are all quite vague, but they can be rather similar among human beings. Then, gradually, some human beings translate those feelings into thoughts, and they would say, "A snake represents a kind of flexible slipping through life with wisdom." These are crude ways to put this, but it shows you how human beings eventually, using their intellect, create meanings for symbols that can be generalized among some human beings. You often consider such generalizations to be an "archetype."

In creating such symbolic understandings, the intellectual descriptions of the symbols are the end of the process. The actual meaning is felt, it is intuitive, it is an internal kind of response. So, there is a very vague and amorphous intellectual structure, or a structure with holes in it, that loosely links the human interpretation of symbols.

QUESTION: You said that our understanding and our use of symbols are somewhat immature. How can we mature our use of symbols?

It is by the knowledge of your own human personality. It is by the personal growth of you as an individual, in relation to your understanding of, and response to symbols.

For example, let us say that you would see a cross used in the Christian tradition, and, inwardly, you would feel, from a certain negative experience that you have had with a religious grouping, a sense of *discomfort*. Let us say that you translate that feeling of discomfort into an intellectual response that says: "This cross represents to me, ignorance, ones who are narrow in their religious beliefs, ones who wish to force their beliefs upon me."

Now, you could say in your *mind* that this cross represents ignorance, but, in your *feelings*, it represents discomfort, fear, a sense of impotence associated with a fear that others can overpower you—many different things. If you do not grow and see what feelings you have in relation to that symbol, then you have an immature interpretation that the cross stands for ignorance. But, if you see all of those emotional patterns inside you, then you could say, "To me, the cross stands for all of these uncomfortable emotional patterns that it stirs inside me."

If you can then extend your knowing beyond yourself, and you can come to know the ones of the Christian tradition who hold that symbol dear—and, in your ignorance, you have dismissed them as too narrow—then you can come to know that some of them have an extremely deep commitment to God. And this symbol to them represents purity, magnificence, and goodness. By realizing this, you have extended your understanding of symbols even further, beyond your personal realm, into the subjective realm of others.

Then, if you persist in taking periods of time to open yourself to feeling the eternal truths of life, and the eternal realities, gradually you can begin to have some deep inner experiences that you can begin to apply to symbols.

For example, let us consider the word symbol, *God*. And let us say that you have only felt frustration when you try to feel what God is. That would be an immature response to that symbol. Then, let us say, over a number of years, you penetrate deeply into your heart, and you begin to feel the truth of God as an extraordinary force of love and creativity that fills you day after day. Now, your response to the word symbol *God* is very large, and varied, and multifaceted, and complex.

When each of you do that kind of inner work individually, then, in your communications to one another about life and about symbols, you will have a richer communication. You will stimulate new meanings and ideas in one another. And, from the personal evolution of *individuals*, there will come about the evolution of the entire race in its use of symbols.

QUESTION: How has the advent of television and movies affected our creative imagination and the symbols from our unconscious minds?

Let us say that you are one who must feed many children, and you desire to feed them healthy food. But, every day, for reasons that live inside you—let us say that you are frugal, you are trying to save money—you feed them only hamburgers. Now, hamburgers are not bad, but they are not the only food, and they are not a wide enough range of food. In general, you ones tend to feed one another, through your communication media, and particularly through the screens where you have images and sounds, the content that is in a narrow range. It is content that is most immediate to the individuals who *create* that content.

In other words, if one who makes the television productions believes that humans like crime, then, to succeed—primarily out of a personal desire for money, stature, and wealth for himself or herself—that one will create productions about crime. And, you ones eat those hamburgers. If the ones who create those productions do not have a gentle sensitivity toward other areas of life, and if they are motivated only by the need to succeed, they will feed you hamburgers until you say, "No more hamburgers."

So, because of the narrow range, there is a distortion of symbols through your media. But, you are free to respond in a broader way to narrowed symbols that you ones create in your media. You are free to shake off the hamburgers, and take the bread and go forth and make a different thing out it. Perhaps to put some cheese in the sandwich, or many different things.

Although your media can tend to be oppressive for your children, squeezing them into narrower thoughts and feelings about the symbols of life than might be desired by the souls of those children, the souls have an understanding of your movement, and they have accounted for it. The souls have placed into the personalities of this generation of children, greater intelligence and greater sensitivity so that they can cope more successfully with the distortion created by your human communication media.

In general, the distortion of your media leans toward an over-focus upon areas that are too *intense*, that stimulate excitement, diversion, and entertainment. Those have their value, of course, but when that is all that you do, then you are eating hamburgers. They are not bad, but there needs to be more variety.

So, the way that you presently use symbols in your media tends to either squeeze a human being and encourage them to be less than they could be, or, if they are intelligent, it stimulates them to realize that they need to expand inside themselves. What they are being fed by the media is not large enough.

QUESTION: Where does our dream symbolism come from?

Here is a rather different area, although similar to the waking use of the mind in symbolizing. But, in this case, since your personality is not fully in control—it is only, in a way, unconsciously in control—in the dream state there is usually less distortion, less of the human miscalculation and confusion, and less impact from human negativity, although it still exists.

In the waking state, you are aware only of what enters your conscious mind. That is the nature of human life. You have your resistances and your controls, your barriers and your blockages, and all of the personality inhibitions to seeing deeper and understanding deeper. So, you will tend to translate your symbols quite literally. But, when you are sleeping, your control is loosened, and many of your distortions are not activated—although some of them can be.

In your sleep there is usually a blank period, if you are not hyperactive, or overstimulated by such things as food, or caffeine, or the excitement of the day. If you are a normal, calm, healthy human being, you enter into a blank sleep period during which there is no personality control. Your temporary human personality package is put aside. It momentarily vanishes. Speaking quite crudely, your personality package is "taken into" the eternal soul that is you—that has created your present personality.

As the personality package is taken back by you-as-a-soul, in a way, it is taught. It is infused with stimulating energies and forces which, in human terms, would need to be called *ideas* and *feelings*, although the thoughts and feelings of souls are quite different. Thus, your personality package is stimulated in certain directions that are important for the soul. But, you-as-a-human are not aware of any of this. You are blank in your human awareness. Otherwise, these adjustments could not be accomplished, for your human awareness would overwatch and distort with its rigid patterns that it has learned from this lifetime.

When the blank sleep period begins to end, again crudely speaking, your soul needs to make your human awareness aware of what the soul has striven to implant and teach. So, gradually, as your human awareness returns in your sleep, and as your mind again becomes active—and even the feelings are activated in dreams—there is created an experience, which is a dream.

The teaching given by your soul to your personality during the blank sleep period is done by eternal forces of your soul. Those forces cannot be perceived by human beings because they are what you would call "energies" of an entirely different nature. In order for you to become aware of the eternal forces that have taught you, those forces need to have some *shape*, some *form*. They need to be clothed in something that your human personality can recognize, something made of the stuff of human life. They need to turn into such things as people, places, events, thoughts, and feelings in order for you to be aware that you have been taught.

Here is where the human personality takes partial control again. Let us say that you are frightened of poverty. During the blank sleeping period before you begin to dream, your soul would give you energies and teachings that would say these realities: "The forces of God are yours. You will never fall into poverty if you use them." Your soul is trying to show you the power that you have to achieve wealth. Let us say that in order to help you become aware of this, your soul would desire you, in your dream, to see yourself discovering a vast treasure. That treasure is, crudely speaking, the *symbol* that your soul would hope that you would create in your dream. Therefore, your soul gives you an impulse to create that symbol.

But, let us say that, because you are so frightened of poverty, unconsciously you translate that symbol into a dream of visiting a neighbor who has a vast treasure, but will give you none. You dream that you die of hunger because you are so poor. Those confused dream symbols are created by you, under the influence of a soul impulse that intended for you to inspire yourself with that dream. But, because your fear of poverty was so great, and had not been grappled with and healed by you in a conscious state, you unintentionally translated the dream symbols into areas that stirred up more fear.

This has a beneficial effect if you let yourself be frightened by the dream. Then, the same purpose would be accomplished, for you would see: "I have many fears about wealth and poverty. I need to heal them." If you begin to heal your fears, then you open the door to feel those soul impulses that say to you: "The forces of God are yours. Use them to create wealth."

This example can give you a feeling for dream symbolism, in a general way.

QUESTION: How do our past life images influence the present, in terms of the symbols that we are drawn to?

It is similar to the present life. If you are very fond of horses in the present, and the symbol of a horse stirs in you feelings of joy, then that can trigger unconscious memories of past times in which horses have been associated with joy. You will stir up those energies from the past, and you will bring them into the present. You will unconsciously amplify your present response to certain symbols by adding the energy of the joy that you had with those symbols in past lifetimes.

To clarify this, let us say that you are a religious person in the Buddhist tradition, and you would have a small statue of the Buddha before you. Others would see that statue, and to them it would simply be an interesting object. But, to you, because you are religious, it is a symbol that stirs feelings of enlightenment, and of God. If you had no past times on earth in the Buddhist tradition, then you would perhaps have a moderately deep experience before that statue in the present. However, if you had walked with the Buddha himself in the past, or if you had transformed your life by following that pathway in subsequent lifetimes, then those past energies would unconsciously combine with your present willingness to venerate the Buddha, and they would give you an extremely deep experience in response to this symbolic representation of the Buddha.

This will essentially apply in many general areas, intellectually, emotionally, even viscerally. For example, let us say that in a past time of earth you were executed by beheading. And, in the present, each time you see a sharp knife your stomach turns. That symbol stirs very deep fears, dreads, and terrors from past lifetimes. When this happens, of course, it is always beneficial to invite the feelings to the surface, for those feelings would not stir in you if they did not need healing. You would need to speak about and share the negative feelings.

There are many positive areas from your past lifetimes that you can be inspired by. If you are deeply touched by the sight of a rose, perhaps you were one of the brotherhood of the Rosy Cross, and that symbol to you represents the extraordinary love and power of the Christ. When you feel a positive stirring such as that, you need to encourage it, and expand it, and work with it.

The *negative* stirrings from the past times of earth associated with symbols need to encourage you to bring your fears to the surface and heal them. The *positive* stirrings need to encourage you to expand upon the creativity and love inherent in those symbols.

QUESTION: It seems that anything in our life that is manifest, that is seen, that is physical or material, can serve as a symbol to stir up something inside of us—something unseen and hidden. Is that true?

This is the key to the mystery of life. For in becoming human, you are an eternal soul that is not physical, but a part of you is taking up and animating physical form. When you are in human form and you only perceive physical reality, you cannot clearly perceive truth, because, even though the physical realities are similar in some ways to the invisible forces of souls and God that have created the physical world, the physical reality is not large enough to contain all truth. You can express many things through physical reality, but you can only partially express truth. That is why the human mind and heart are needed. They expand upon the physical reality.

For example, if you see a certain large stone, and you are uninformed and insensitive about certain matters, you would simply say, "Here is a large stone," and you pass by it. But, let us say that you have a great sensitivity in the Christian tradition, and you would say, "Here is the very rock from which Jesus Christ himself ascended into heaven.'' Now you have an extraordinary experience because you have responded to the physical reality of the rock with inner forces, and possibilities, and energies that are triggered by symbolic interpretations of that stone.

So, the symbols, in a way, allow you to *expand* physical reality. If you only literally lived physical reality, you would be very small. Symbolic interpretation of the physical reality opens the door to merging the physical with the spiritual, or eternal. Thus, the way that you use symbols, consciously and unconsciously, can expand your life.

QUESTION: Do our guides, or souls speak to us through symbols? If so, what should we be alert to ''hear'' from them?

The clearest ''speaking'' to you from guiding ones and from your soul is done through *feelings*. But, generally, your feelings are so saturated with human emotion, and the complexities of the physical world, that you cannot notice the very subtle forces of spiritual reality entwining into your feelings. So, even though feelings are the clearest way to ''hear'' guiding ones, and souls, and God, hearing through feeling is usually most difficult, for human ones rarely take the time to calm their feelings enough to become that smooth pool that can reflect the reality beyond it, and not within it.

Most human ones, trained in the earth ways of *intensity*, which involves dramatic events experienced in sense perceptible ways, will usually expect to inwardly *see* the symbols and images given to them by guiding ones. Those who prefer word symbols, and who are intellectually inclined rather than visually inclined, expect to *hear* words in their ears from guiding ones. But, your *feelings* are where the eternal beings focus most of their energy. Yet, your ordinary human emotions are very strong and intense, and they usually obscure the guidance being given to you in your feelings.

The eternal beings are trying to help you *feel* the truth, for that is the clearest way to circumvent your own human prejudices and interpretations of symbols. When you *feel* God, there is no ambiguity about it. You know you are feeling God. When you *think* about God, there is much ambiguity. You could think that God is many things—an energy, a light, a force, a being, a horse—whatever pleases you. The feeling of God is unambiguous. It is direct, it is real, it is true.

The eternal forces try to communicate with you through your feelings. But, human beings, being rather willful and stubborn, and fascinated by dramatic sensual input, look for images, words, sounds, and so forth.

This is not to say that the eternal forces do not permeate your thinking, and seeing, and so forth. But, those areas are even more dominated by physical reality than are your feelings. Most of you have never seen anything but physical objects, or your imaginations of physical things. Most of you have never heard anything but audible sounds. You are so indoctrinated in the physical perceptions that the eternal forces simply cannot be dramatic enough to get your attention.

If you do succeed in, let us say, having a vision that is a partial perception of forces being given to you by your soul, your personality is so strong that it will dominate what that vision becomes. For example, let us say that you are meditating. Then, if you see images in your meditation, it will be similar to your dream images—and even more so because you are conscious. You will tend to see what *you* desire to see, not what your *soul* desires to show you. You will tend to *interpret* what your guidance is attempting to communicate. Usually, you will do this unconsciously, by creating the symbols that you expect. If you are a follower of Confucius, you will see Confucius. Thus, even when you attain a deep state of attunement and are truly drawing upon your spiritual guidance, the symbols that you perceive, even verbal interpretations and inputs, will generally be a product of your own personality. This does not mean that those symbols are useless. They can be very beneficial. But, you would caution yourself against taking them literally. Symbols are very flexible, and they will change greatly throughout your life.

QUESTION: Would you give us a guided meditation, or method, that we can use to help awaken the creative richness within us, and to reawaken that capacity to know God through our intuition and feelings?

First of all, each of you would need to dedicate yourselves sincerely to such a process. You would not gain much simply by dabbling in it.

For those of you who have a deep longing to know the truth about life, and to bring it forth as clearer understanding in your mind, in your vision, in your hearing, in your feeling, then the area of symbols is extremely rich. It can bring forth a greater understanding of God.

We would suggest the following method as one that can be a starting point for you. As you learn from it and with it, you can make your own refinements and your own adjustments as you go along.

Of course, first of all, there needs to be silence, and withdrawal from the distractions of the physical world. This means that you need a time set aside, and a private place where you can release your worries and concerns of the physical life. You would set aside that time in each day

As you enter that period, begin the releasing process by saying to yourself:

"In this moment, my affairs of earth are put aside, and I do not need to give attention to them. They are behind me now. And, as I sit here, I am releasing my personality from the franticness of its earth pursuits.

As I sit and begin to relax my physical body, I am beginning a process of release of the limits to my perceptions. I bless my human perceptions. They help me master earth, which is one of my purposes. But, it is not my purpose to be dominated by those perceptions, for I am much more than my human perceptions. I am much more than my thoughts, and feelings, and actions in this

**world. They are very important, but they are only
a part of me. And, in this moment, in order to feel
and perceive the rest of me, I put aside this domi-
nating intensity, and I release."**

Gently, as you continue to relax your body as best you
can, you will still your mind and soothe your feelings.
Encourage feelings of warmth, and peace, and love. Do
this for as long as you feel you need to, knowing that the
critical part of your mind will usually say, "This is not
good enough or perfect enough." Simply ignore that and
move on.

Next, after you have attained a relatively peaceful
state, you would say:

**"In this moment, I turn myself to God. I do not
need to see what God is, or even be able to think
what God is. I give myself to the *feeling* of God."**

At first, as a starting point, you might gently define
God for yourself. For example, you might say, "God is
feelings of love and perfection." Then, gently imagine
those feelings. Encourage them inside you, but inwardly
say:

"I give myself to God."

All of this is your creative part. So far, you have used
your *will* as a human being to make *choices*. First, you
chose to put aside your personality domination. Next, you
chose to give yourself to God. Up to this point, you have
been willful. You have been *doing*, inwardly. Now, you
will begin to *not* do.

This step can be difficult, but you will learn to attain it. After you have given yourself to God, you would say:

"Now, God itself guides me."

Then, you release, and you float. In time, you will be carried into areas of understanding. At times, your thoughts and feelings might nag at you. Simply continue to release and ignore them. Continue to give yourself to God. And, continue, as best you can, to try not to do. You are doing nothing now. You are being carried by God. You are being given to. You are being expanded. You are being infused with truth.

This might be a blank period. Do not try to create images and thoughts. After you have launched those initial feelings that to you represent God, do not even try to create feelings. Simply release, and trust, and know that God will love you and guide you.

Do that for as long as you desire, as long as it pleases you. Do not be concerned with what you are observing. Simply continue releasing.

When you decide that it is time to end this period of being guided by God—in which there may be no content at all for your mind or your feelings—you would gently say:

"Now, I open my heart, and I again take willful control of my personality. I ask that God, and my guiding ones, and my soul, stimulate in me now, the images, the feelings, the thoughts, the words, or the symbols that are most important to me as I move through this lifetime—that relate to my

most important purposes. **I am requesting these,
knowing that I am worthy of having them, that I
am a magnificent human being who loves life and
God, who has given myself to God during this silent period. I ask for benefit to my personality in
the form of knowledge, and input, and symbols.''**

Then, make a silent period. Let images, or thoughts, or
words, or feelings begin to bubble into your awareness, to
the surface of your awareness—not so much controlling
them, simply *inviting* them. Simply observe, and notice,
and let these areas unfold naturally, as best you can.

After you feel that you have done this for as long as
you wish, you would very slowly, very gently bring yourself back to your conscious alertness in your human life.
Then, immediately begin to write on paper all that you
can remember about the images, or the words, or the
feelings, or the sounds that you received.

After you do this attunement for a period of time, you
will begin to wish to interpret, and make some learning.
Do it easily, slowly. This is a way to use your creative
capacity to translate invisible, eternal forces into tangible
reality through symbolic understanding.

For the moment, imagine that you have done this attunement successfully. Imagine that you are now surrounded by love. Imagine that your feelings are so joyful
because you have made this connection. You now feel, ''I
am not alone in earth. I am loved by God itself, by my
own soul, by many other souls. I am loved by many hu-

man beings. But, these forces of love are invisible until I turn them into feelings.''

Do that now, as best you can, as you are inwardly guided in this moment. Turn the forces of God into feelings of love inside you, and rejoice in them. And, as you do it in this moment, you can do it in any moment in the future, whenever it pleases you.

Release yourself then into this love. Let it stir the wonderful feelings inside you, and use those feelings to lift yourself and others, throughout this lifetime.

Chapter Two

THE HUMAN MIND

Exploring the Mystery of Consciousness

In order to look clearly at the human mind as it presently exists within you ones of earth, there is a need for a preliminary understanding of that which would be your experience *before* there was a mind to have inside you. So, let us begin with a look at the early stages of the earth, during a period in which the eternal souls established the physical forms that you would understand as the planets, the stars, and the universe.

At that time, the structure of the physical universe would be as you now observe it. But, in the human forms, there would not be physical human bodies as you now know them. There would simply be certain "energy patterns" floating about, and those patterns would not have physical shape, or *form*. Let us call these human energy patterns a *personality matrix*.

In the early stages of life, before there was the present human physical body for the personality matrix to be put into, we could say that the souls themselves were "practicing" projecting *portions* of themselves as energy forces. It would be as though you have a light shining upon a wall, and you are practicing making a shadow of a horse's head with your hands. This would give you an idea of the *shape* of a horse's head. Those souls who would eventually create human bodies, as you now know them, would practice projecting, if you will, *shadows of themselves upon the ether*, or upon the *energies* of time and space. In this way, they would create a beginning personality matrix for themselves. They would do this by putting together energies of certain *feelings* and *awarenesses*. These energies would be prepared by the souls to go *inside* the evolving physical bodies that would eventually become the present human bodies that you know of.

In the early expressions of *non-physical* human beings, *you*, as an eternal soul, could express a portion of yourself as a human personality matrix floating freely around earth. That personality matrix would be aware of earth, would have perceptions that are similar to your present physical perceptions—in terms of *seeing* earth, *hearing* it, and so forth—and yet, there would be a kind of "mirror" sense to your personality experience. You would know that your human personality experience was just a *projection*. In other words, you as a personality would not *believe in* your earth experience, just as you would not believe that the shadow of a horse's head made by your hands is a real horse.

Now, let us imagine that the shadow of the horse's head had some *self awareness*. It would *feel* itself as a reflection of your hands. So, it would now say, "I am a shadow of a horse's head. I am those hands *projected into another dimension of reality*. And I am smaller than those hands." In the same way, as the first non-physical personality projection of you, you would feel, "I am a projection of energies from the soul into the physical dimension."

However, these kinds of personality awarenesses would not be like your present clear thinking. They would be rather fuzzy, and cloudy, and intuitive—a very vague sensing, primarily dominated by your *eternal* awareness of yourself as a soul. In other words, the *human personality awareness* of you on earth would not be so clear and independent. You would feel, primarily, "*I am an eternal soul projecting a portion of myself into a human personality matrix.*"

You would feel this by using certain processes taking place inside your eternal being, processes that are similar to your present *thinking* abilities, but, they would be so much larger, broader, sharper, and clearer than human thoughts. They would be so much informed with forces of *love* and *wisdom* that they would overshadow your awareness of yourself as a human personality.

In those early stages of existence when the human personality matrix floated about without a body, you would have, so to speak, a crude, "amoebae-like" sensing of the *physical* world. Your *primary* awareness would be held in you as an eternal soul. Then, gradually, over great periods of time, as you ones as souls were able to fit your personality matrix *into* the early physical bodies, there would eventually come about beings similar to present physical human beings.

However, those early human beings would be extremely *dense*, mentally and intellectually. In other words, there would be a *formative mind* in those human beings that would be very vague, not clear, not precise. That is because most of the awareness in that physical human being would be: "I am a projection of an eternal soul, and I am that soul."

At first, because of that awareness of the soul in the physical human beings, there would be very little interest in the physical world, apart from simple animal pleasures of attraction and repulsion. Since most of the awareness in that early human personality would be of its eternal nature, the workings of the human mind would be vague, crude, and not so intelligent. This would be the precursor of the present human mind. The fledgling intellectual forces that would later come to be the fully developed human mind would be very weak in those early humans on earth, because the mental energies of those early personalities were so overshadowed by *intuitive* sensings and perceptions of the eternal worlds. Such intuitive perceptions are not made with the *mind*, but with an inner sensitivity that is a *feeling*.

Over a great period of time, as humans would interact with the physical world, pay more attention to it, grapple with it, and begin to master it, the human mind would grow. During that period, generation after generation, the energies that began as those very simple mental forces would coalesce, become stronger and more precise, and would be intensified by human learning and experience carried from lifetime to lifetime. The result was that the human mind in each individual would, in subsequent lifetimes, grow stronger and more potent. The mind would become more complex and diversified, more brilliant. This has led up to the present modern period in which you are now mastering the physical world *because* of the brilliance of the human mind.

From this you can understand that the mind is not an *object*. It is a living conglomeration of *forces* and *energies* that have evolved from the beginning of human time—from a very weak spark, into a brilliant flame that now lives in most human beings, except for those in whom the souls have chosen, for their own reasons, to suppress the brilliance of the mind.

QUESTION: Would you give a definition of the human mind, and explain how it works to enable human beings to think?

To understand this for this time, say to yourself: "The human mind is a collection of *forces* and *energies* that are eternal." Those forces are woven into a certain *structure* for you by your soul.

To help you feel this more clearly, let us say that you have long reeds of dried grass. You weave those reeds into a basket. You still have *only* dried grass, but the grass now has a *structure* that you can define as something *more* than the dried grass. You can now call the reeds of grass a *basket*.

In a similar way, the human mind is woven of energies. Those energies come together inside your personality matrix and they conglomerate about *your sense of yourself*. Fed into those energies by your soul are unconscious memories of your past lifetimes on earth. Your soul also feeds into those energies a great deal of knowledge that you have gained through many human lifetimes. There is also some knowledge of *eternal* worlds, which usually is unconscious. All of these are energies—the reeds of grass. These energies are woven together in your personality matrix inside your body to create a *structure* that is a human mind—the basket.

Now, imagine weaving a basket that can *grow*. The human mind is an *energy structure* that can grow. The mind can know that it has been fed from past knowledge, and, it can continually create *new* knowledge by perceiving the physical world, and by *propagating itself* by its own thinking. In other words, in a way, the more you think, the larger your mind becomes. The more complex your thinking, the more complex your mind. If you think only simple thoughts for a lifetime, your mind does not complexify as much as if you ponder complex and varied thoughts. So, the human mind is a growing kind of energy structure that lives inside you.

Usually, you identify *yourself* as your mind. Most of you tend to think, "I am my mind." However, at the same time, you might think, "I am also my body, and my feelings.'' When you have such responses, you begin to sense that your mind is not an *isolated* energy structure. In other words, your mind is not the only energy structure woven from eternal energies that you have in your personality matrix. There is more that one basket woven from the grass.

Let us say that there is a *collection* of baskets, contained within a larger basket. Your *mind* is one basket. Your *emotions* are another. Your *beliefs* are another. Your *images* are another. Your physical perceptions, such as what you see and hear, are another. This goes on and on. The mind is only one stream of energies inside your personality matrix. It is one basket. Put it with all of the other baskets, ''group'' them together, and you have a large basket that contains the small ones. That large basket is your *personality matrix*. Temporarily, while you are a human being, *you* are essentially your personality matrix.

So, inside the whole energy structure of your personality matrix, there is your thinking stream of energies, your feeling energies, your idea energies, your sense of self energies, and all of the other energy structures that live within your human experience. But, we could say that the *mind* is one of the ''largest'' energy structures, for it does tend to dominate most of the other energies inside of you.

This domination of the mind is *intended* by the souls. The mind is your key to moving about within human life. For the most part, you will *think* your way through life. You will use your mind to be aware of life, and to live it.

Human *feelings* are also strong, and they will influence

your thinking, just as your thinking influences your feelings. The two larger energy streams in your personality matrix are thinking and feeling.

For simplicity, the human mind can be seen as several *different* configurations of mental energy. For example, you could sit staring at a wall, and there is no thought in you. For that moment, your mind is only your *vision* of that wall. At a different time, you could be thinking of many complex ideas. For that moment, your mind is all of those ideas. So, the first configuration of mental energy is *your conscious mind*, and what you are consciously aware of in any moment, which can be extremely small. You can, at times, be almost aware of nothing. Let us say that your conscious mind is your *working mind*—the one that is doing the work through conscious awareness.

The next state, or configuration of your mind would be *all that you have even been consciously aware of*. This would include everything that you have ever *consciously* known or experienced, such as the face of your mother, a blue sky, words spoken to you by other people, thoughts that you have had, feelings that you have had. This includes all of your awareness of yourself, and your awareness of all of your inner streams of experience throughout this lifetime, some of which you can recall at will, and some of which you have temporarily forgotten—experiences that in the past were fully in your conscious mind, but now you have set them aside. In this moment, you are not thinking about all of the thoughts that you have had throughout this lifetime, but most of those areas are readily available to you.

This configuration of your mind is composed of a wide variety of many different things, and this mind lives just beneath the surface of your conscious awareness. Without entering into complex psychological terminology, we could say that this configuration of your mind is the "reservoir" of the conscious mind. It is not unconscious, in the sense that it is hidden, or inaccessible to you. It is simply the reservoir of past conscious knowledge that you can call upon at any moment. Essentially, it is conscious to you, although you are not holding it in your moment to moment awareness.

Then, to simplify the complexity, we could say that there is a capacity to "put things away for good," for an entire lifetime. Such things are still in your mental energies, but they will not arise spontaneously. In a very general way of speaking, you could understand this as the *unconscious mind*. These are the things that you *could* know in your mind, but, most likely, you shall not, unless you dig for them. These could include long lost memories and deeply rooted thoughts and feelings that have been pushed from consciousness and are not accessible to you. They could include many things that live in you as *potential*, but most likely will not be brought to your conscious awareness unless you do some work to stimulate that larger reservoir which is your unconscious mind.

There is also a deeper level of the unconscious mind that includes all of your memories of all of the many past lifetimes that you have lived on earth. The energies of those memories are less strong and less tangible than unconscious energies from your present lifetime. Because they were not intended to be a large conscious part of your life, and they were intended to work upon your personality without you noticing them, they have been "constructed" of more refined energies. They are simply held within your personality matrix as finer energies. Of course, your conscious and unconscious minds work together, and they can interact if you set your will to it. Therefore, you can learn to intentionally open the unconscious reservoirs and invite more of the memories of past lifetimes to the surface. If you are persistent, you might draw some of them into your conscious awareness.

This is a very simple and crude way for you to understand the mind as a construct of energies, some of which are available to you consciously, while others are not. The human mind is a constantly fluctuating, growing structure, with energies coming into it from beyond earth, and, unconsciously, from other human beings on earth. There are also the energies coming into your mind from your conscious day to day experience. So, rather than visualizing the mind as a house with one person in it, it would be closer to the reality of the mind to visualize it as a large train station with many people constantly going in and out.

QUESTION: What is the relationship between the mind and the brain?

To take a step toward understanding the relationship between the mind and the brain, imagine a Ping-Pong ball in the middle of a vicious game. The ball is being smashed to and fro. Now, let us imagine that the Ping-Pong ball is aware of itself, but has no *vision*. It knows that it is moving back and forth rapidly, but it has no idea *why*. It cannot *see* the paddles that are making it move.

In a certain sense, as present human beings, you ones have been projected forth by your souls in a way that you do not see. You simply know that you are moving through life. You did not see the "paddle" of the soul strike you, so to speak, and set you into motion. You certainly did not see, and become aware of the fact that your personality has been created by an eternal soul, nor did you see how you have been projected into a human body that is physical.

However, *before* you entered your body at birth, you had an awareness, and, essentially, a mind, and all of your personality matrix energies. You *were* aware of your eternal soul having created you. In essence, before your birth, your awareness was an *energy structure* floating "outside" of your fetus form.

Now, here it becomes a bit confusing, but, to put it simply, while your fetus form is growing in your mother's womb, you, as a personality matrix of energies, are experimenting with moving some parts of your fetus body. The fetus form has an *animal* life of its own, and if you as a personality matrix did not enter that body, it could be born physically, and survive for a while without you inside it. Before birth, it could move about in the womb without you paying any attention to it. But, most personality matrices, before they enter into the physical body after birth, will "practice" a bit before the birth. In a crude way of speaking, they will float around the fetus form and try to merge with the "electrical circuitry" of the *brain* of the fetus form that is, instinctively, in an animal way, moving some of the fetus body.

So, you, as a personality matrix, might begin a preliminary engagement with the brain of that fetus body, which is simply an animal physiological structure that has no awareness of itself. It does not think. It simply responds in instinctive ways.

Generally, for most human beings, shortly after the birth of the fetus form, the personality matrix is plunged into the physical body. The *mind* energy structure that existed in the personality matrix *before* the birth of the body will rather rapidly—in one day, or several weeks, depending upon the individual—stimulate the physical *brain* of the newborn child and cause an extraordinary, miraculous explosion of what you would call, *self awareness*. This explosion of self awareness, crudely speaking, transforms the newborn child from an animal into a human.

In that explosion of self awareness, the *mind energy structure* of the personality matrix, which is composed of the energies woven by the soul from divine forces of God, impregnates the physical brain of the child body. *Those divine energies literally cause the cells of the physical brain to explode*, in terms of the *energy* in the cells. The exploding energies accelerate the physiological structure of the brain. If you looked at the brain after this acceleration, objectively, it would look the same. You would not see a change. Yet, all of the extraordinary forces that you

call *electrical* and *chemical* forces, that you believe originate thought, would be stimulated into action. Those
forces would begin to give the brain the ability to *mirror*
thought.

In other words, the *thinking* is actually done by the
eternal forces that are woven into your *mind*, or *your
mental energy structure* that lives inside your personality
matrix. But, after you enter your physical body, that energy of thought impregnates the brain and causes the brain
to *mirror* the thoughts that are originating in your personality matrix of energies. *The non-physical, mental energies of the personality matrix are transformed into
physical brain energies.*

While you are in human form, you will need your
brain to think. If your brain becomes damaged, unless you
leave your body, you will not be aware that you are
thinking or perceiving. That is why there is the illusion
that the brain *is* the mind.

In a sense, at your physical birth, you *transfer* the
thinking "mechanisms" of your personality matrix to
your physical brain. Your brain *mirrors* those mechanisms
and *feeds them back to your human awareness*. Generally,
unless you make a mystical disconnection from your
body, or you elevate your consciousness to heightened
states, or you come into what you would call a *near-death*
experience, the brain of your body will, for all intents and
purposes, create the thinking processes, or, more accurately put, it will take over the *mirroring* of the thinking
processes while the mind energies in your personality matrix, which are not physical, will still *originate* the

thoughts.

Even when you are in physical form, your non-physical mind is still your mind, and it will still do the thinking. In a way, your non-physical mind *directs* the physical brain. While you are in your body, you will not be aware of your non-physical mind. That mind will direct your brain, and it is your brain that will give you your conscious experience of *human mind*. But, your *real* mind is larger than your brain.

At death, again speaking quite crudely, a reverse process occurs. The physical brain dies, and it releases its *mirroring* function. So, you no longer feel, "I am thinking in my head," for you do not have a physical head. The physical body is dead, and now you feel, "I am thinking inside *me*. And me is not a physical body. Me is a presence. Me is an energy matrix."

Briefly, after your death, you think primarily through your personality matrix of energies. But, very quickly, almost instantly for some, you again become aware that you are an eternal soul, and you realize that *you are thinking through eternal forces of God that are unlimited*. Your mind then, in essence, returns to an awareness of what could be called "the mind of God."

Now, *always* you are linked to the mind of God, whether you are alive in a physical body, or existing apart from a body. The forces of life that you could call many things—love, mental energy, power, beauty, goodness—all of those forces emanate from what you would call God, which is an extraordinary presence and reality. You could call some of those eternal forces "the mind of

God." These are particular forces that you as a soul experience as *the awareness of God*. However, the forces of God have created souls who have their own awareness of themselves as eternal beings. Thus, you might consider this soul awareness to be a "smaller" version of the mind of God. Then, the *human* mind can be considered to be a "smaller" version of the mind of the soul. Therefore, the human mind can also be considered to be part of the mind of God.

When you make your physical death, your brain gives up its mirroring function, and you cease to feel that you are thinking with your brain inside your physical head. Gradually, you begin to realize, "I am thinking, and I am being aware of realities through my eternal existence, my eternal awareness, which is an expression of God."

This is a simple way to relate to you some of the complexities of the relationship between the mind and the physical brain.

QUESTION: When we think, there seems to be an observer in the system. We feel, "I am aware of my own thinking." What is the "I" in us that observes our thoughts? Is it the personality matrix that you were speaking of?

In order to understand this area of experiencing, imagine that you have a straight line laid out horizontally in front of you, and the left end of the line represents the "I" that you experience when you are a personality matrix hovering about your fetus body just before its birth. Then, as you move along the line to the right, there is a point on the line that represents the birth of your physical body. Before that birth, at the left end of the line, you are an "I" with an awareness of yourself as a non-physical personality matrix, and you are also clearly aware that you are projected from an eternal soul.

Once you cross the point on the line that represents the birth of your physical body, then, to the right of that point, the line represents *your entire human life*. To the far right of that is another point which represents your physical *death* as a human being. Between the two points that represent your human birth and death, the "I" that you experience as yourself—if you are healthy and normal, mentally, emotionally, and physically—is an experience *reflected off of the brain of your physical body*. While you live inside your physical body, you are still a personality matrix, but you are "observing" your own mental processes, emotional processes, and physical perceptions as they are all reflected into your human awareness by your physical brain.

It is as if you are at the theater. And let us say that you own the theater. The actors are all your relatives, and you have written the play. You have put it all together. All of those extensions of you are carrying out a drama, and *you are witnessing the drama*. In a sense, *you are living yourself*. It is the same in your human life. You are temporarily *being* your human thoughts and feelings, but, you are also aware of them from a slight distance. You are *witnessing* your thoughts, and feelings, and your life. You are the actors on the stage, *living* the drama, and you are the audience, *observing* the drama.

As you live your life each day, you can switch back and forth from *witnessing* your thoughts and feelings in any moment, to *becoming* those thoughts and feelings. When you become your thoughts and feelings, you are no longer observing them, you are simply having them. Then, you can consciously step back from having the thoughts and emotions to your personality observing point, and you can once again *notice* that you are having certain thoughts and feelings. You can be the *experiencer* of yourself. You can be the *observer* of yourself.

When you are the *experiencer* of yourself, you are totally inundated by your mental and emotional energies. To all intents and purposes, you *are* your mind when you are totally lost in your thinking. Then, when you step back to become your whole personality matrix observing yourself, and you notice, "I am thinking this thought," then you are the *observer* of yourself.

While you are alive as a human being, the *you* that you experience is *your personality matrix* that is *temporarily* using your physical body. Even though, many times you may feel like you *are* that body, you are not. You are you *inside* that body. You are the *small* you, which is *self consciousness* created by the personality matrix of energies that has temporarily entered a physical body.

Looking at our line again, when you move to the right and pass the point that represents your human death, at first, immediately after your death, you regain your awareness of yourself as a personality matrix that is independent of the physical body. You realize that your "I" is an energy structure created by an eternal soul. However,

as you move farther to the right, away from the point of
death, you gradually begin to realize, "*I am my soul.*"
You come to the full awareness that the *you* inside your
experience is an eternal soul, which is your eternal nature.

**QUESTION: Hypnosis seems to strongly focus the
mind in one area. How does hypnosis work, and what
does it do to the mind?**

First of all, the repetition of words and thoughts in
hypnosis creates a kind of *resonating* influence upon the
thoughts. So, the more you repeat a thought, an image, or
a statement of your will—whatever you use to reverberate
thoughts and will—the more there is set up a resonance,
or a sympathetic vibration. If the thought were a sound, it
would become louder. Simply speaking, when a thought is
focused upon and repeated intentionally and willfully,
either by you inwardly, or by one who is hypnotizing you
by repeating a theme or a focus, the *energy* of that
thought is amplified. And, generally, in a successful
hypnosis, all other thoughts are temporarily pushed into
the background.

Let us say that there is a female-one who wishes to
have a hypnotist convince her that she is beautiful physically, and she does not believe so, although her physical
form is attractive. In the hypnotic process, she enters into
a physical *relaxation*, which draws physiological stimulations away from the brain. In other words, when you are
not moving physically, or doing, and you are not thinking
and feeling strongly, the signals for those activities are not
occupying the brain. They are not stimulating the brain,

so the brain calms itself somewhat. The normal energies of thinking become less chaotic and less strong.

As the hypnotist would say to this female one, "You are beautiful," and the brain is working in its calmer frequency because of the relaxation involved in the hypnotic process, then the brain can easily fasten upon the thought, "You are beautiful." However, the success of the hypnosis will depend upon the *personality structure* of the female one. Let us say that she is agreeable, because she desires to believe that she is beautiful. She is positively inclined toward the suggestion. Of course, if she were negatively inclined, there would be no hypnotic process, but simply a repetition of a statement that is not accepted by her.

Because this female one is positively inclined toward the suggestion that she is beautiful, she allows the *energy* of that thought, so to speak, to begin to reverberate and increase its "vibration rate." Her mind, focusing on that particular thought, sets up a kind of "loop," in which the thought is fed back into the thinking process, to be thought again, and it is fed back, and the energy circulates and increases.

This thought will automatically stir some feelings in the female one. If she accepts the *feeling* of, "I am beautiful," then the energy of that feeling feeds back into the thoughts. Then the thoughts and the feelings begin to set up a resonating cycle that increases in vibration rate, if you will, although this is a crude way to put it. As a result of this, the *inner experience* of the female one is intensified around the theme, "I am beautiful."

Her mind, when relaxed enough, can actually begin to find *reasons* to believe, "I am beautiful." In other words, her mind is prodded toward organizing past thoughts and beliefs that can reinforce the thought, "I am beautiful."

In terms of *energies*, the hypnotic process is one of refining and amplifying forces so that the *experience* of the individual can more readily accept the thoughts or feelings that are focused upon. Those experiences can be extremely strong and forceful.

In hypnosis, the mind can be used to move the personality toward deeper experiences that are not limited to the present lifetime. If, during hypnosis, ones can stir up unconscious memories of their past lifetimes on earth, at times, the link of the mind and the emotions can leap across the gap from the conscious to the unconscious reservoirs of energies, and, the past experiences can be retrieved and brought into the present awareness.

Many things can be done with the mind when it is relaxed and free from the ordinary distractions of day to day life.

QUESTION: There have been many teachings that say that we create our own reality with our minds. Is that true, and if it is, then how does it work?

In looking to this area, imagine that you have a small child that you would send to fetch water for you. You have a friend with you who has not seen the child come and go, but simply sees that you suddenly have water. The friend would be astounded, and would ask, "How did you bring water to your hand?" You would say, "I sent my child for it." But the friend would say, "I see no child."

In a way, the *forces* of matter, the *particles* of matter, that make up solid substances, including your body, have been brought to you by invisible energies that have been sent out from your soul. So, let us say that those energies are the "children" of your soul. The soul would say, "Go fetch me a physical body." Of course, the energies would create that body through the present system of sexual procreation that you are familiar with. But, nevertheless, from a point at which there was no child, suddenly there is a child—you. You are born. You simply do not see the forces that go and get you, and that create you. (You would attribute the creation of your body to sperm and ovum, but you would not see the *forces* within the procreative process that create *life*.)

You also do not see the forces of the souls that allow a tree to be a tree. When you cut down a tree, those forces allow the molecules of wood to remain together so that you can make a board, and then take many boards and make a table. But, you never stop to ask, "If this board is made of alive moving particles, how is it that they all stay together and remain a board? Why do they not become smoke, as they do if we apply heat to the board?"

All of the mysterious "children"—the forces and energies of eternal souls—that rush about *accomplishing* the physical world, and keeping it in place, are never seen by you. You only see the *results*. You are the neighbor who sees that suddenly a glass of water appears, and you ask, "Where did it come from?"

Since you have agreed, while you are human, to temporarily set aside the ability to see the underlying causes of physical reality—the soul forces that hold physical matter in place—then you accept physical matter as something *outside* of yourself. You do not remember that *you* are one of the souls who is continually pouring forth, *through yourself,* the forces of God that keep the matter of the physical universe in place.

If the souls withdrew their forces of God from the physical world, then, instantly, all physical matter would vanish. Space would vanish. Time would vanish. There would be only the unfolding realms of eternal *experience.*

Since you are one of the souls who is *creating* physical reality, down to its most minute manifestation of subatomic particles, atoms, and molecules, then, of course, you have a certain interplay with matter. But, as a human being, as the personality matrix who has said, "I will enter into this body and navigate it through a human lifetime," you have agreed to put aside your ability to actually *manifest* physical matter out of nothing. So, for all intents and purposes, under normal circumstances, your mind cannot affect matter.

You will master physical matter by *your physical actions.* You can say, "I think I will chop this wood," then, your *body* affects matter, directed by your mind. But, in the sense of "mind over matter," where you might cause a glass to jump from a table with your mental energies, most of you will not manifest those abilities, because they are not important to what you are attempting to accomplish as a human being. It is more important to be able to rise up and pick up a glass with your hand, hold it under a fountain, and take some water to put into your body. Those normal kinds of activities, you might say, are the "intended" purposes of your use of mental energies in this lifetime.

However, because you *are* your soul, and because your mind is linked with the forces of your soul, and of God, under some unusual circumstances, some individuals might project mental energies in such an amplified way that those energies could enter into the molecular structure of physical objects, and, in a sense, move them, or cause them to alter their ordinary path. In the most extreme cases—and most likely you would not see this in the present human life—a human being could, with their mind, invite the molecules of the glass to give up their structure, and the glass would be vaporized. The molecules that make up the glass would cease to be glass molecules, and they could become air molecules. The glass would vanish. These are extraordinary *potentials* that, from your viewpoint, can be seen simply as theoretical ideas, for you will not need to manifest this kind of phenomenon in this lifetime.

QUESTION: What about using our minds to create our physical reality, such as through the use of affirmations? If we are using affirmations to create wealth, or health, or some other physical fulfillment, how does our mind accomplish this?

Here is, potentially, a great, powerful use of the human mind. But, it is not yet fully understood, and is therefore difficult to accomplish.

First of all, the mind is powerful in the ordinary manner, with which you are familiar, as when you say, "I am thinking it would be nice to have wealth," and you motivate yourself by such thoughts to work and to multiply your money. Or you might say, "I am thinking that I desire a mating one," and you respond to such thoughts by motivating yourself to go forth to meet others, to fall in love, and to make a marriage.

Often, in your daily life, your mental energies are weakened because your *attention* is divided. Your mind must grapple with many things. You can adjust for this when you take some time to intently focus your mind upon one thing. When you create such a single focus, not only do you stimulate your ordinary desires to do, and to accomplish, but you actually release creative forces and energies inside yourself that *increase* your capacity to successfully act in the physical world, according to your thoughts and your will.

If you sit in silence and say, "I will use my mind to manifest money," and you do only *mental* procedures to focus upon money, you will sit for a long time before the money comes marching into your room and leaps into your hand. Such unusual events will not likely occur in this lifetime.

However, the repetition of your focus mentally, such as when you think, "I desire money," can be helpful in your physical manifestation. This is particularly true if you are confident that you are worthy of having money, and you believe that you can have it. If you believe, "I am an expression of God in human form, and I can have what I desire," such inner activity will usually prompt your personality to do what is needed in the physical world in order to create wealth.

Thus, for most human beings, working with the mind alone is usually not enough to attain what they desire in the physical world. The physical *doing* is also necessary.

However, focusing mentally upon a desire, such as a desire for money, *does intensify energies that flow between yourselves and other human beings.* If you work lovingly and confidently with your thoughts of money, and you circulate among other human beings, in a way, you "magnetize" yourself in a manner that can draw you close to ones who can help you create money, either by partnerships or other interactions.

There are also creative forces that stream forth from your soul, and when you think, "I desire money and shall now create it," and you do it lovingly and confidently, then those creative soul forces are intensified within your personality matrix. Because of those forces, you can have more brilliant ideas. You can have more impactful, creative energies to use to carry out your fulfillment in the physical world.

When you think, "I am worthy of money," you also make *emotional* openings. You soften your personality. You help yourself pass through any obstacles to fulfillment that might be caused by fear and doubt.

The focus upon thoughts does many different things that can help you achieve what you desire in the physical world. The mind can be of great power in these areas.

QUESTION: How is the mind involved in extra sensory perception, such as telepathy and other psychic phenomena?

To simplify many complex areas, we would say that, beneath the conscious level, there is a *constant communication* between all human beings living on the face of the earth. Since such communication is hidden from your ordinary awareness, most of you will never perceive it. However, when you are able to make certain adjustments to your mind, or when certain unusual events occur, in a sense, you can enter into that extraordinary web of human communication and become aware of parts of it.

Let us say that you are a mother, and your daughter is in danger many miles away. Her fear is so strong that when she cries out for you, her thoughts "leap out" of that unconscious web of communication that exists between all human beings, and the energy of her thought becomes tangible enough for you to actually think, "She is in danger." Or, you might *feel* the danger.

In another way of approaching this example, you might *initiate* the action of trying to attune to this deeper level of communication. You might say, "My daughter is at a great distance. I wish to sense how she is." And you make a very deep attunement within yourself, putting aside the distractions of your ordinary earth life. You let your mind expand so that it can penetrate some of those unconscious communications that link you to her through time and space. As your mind penetrates to a deeper level, you may not precisely hear her thoughts, but from her thoughts and feelings you might perceive that she is in danger.

This is a simple illustration, but it shows you that, essentially, when the human mind works in a way that you would consider to be extraordinary, or psychic, or beyond the normal, the mind is simply entering that unconscious level where there is communication between all human beings concerning everything that involves human life.

This unconscious level of communication is also penetrated by forces of the soul. If you could enter this arena of communication deeply enough, you would come to be aware of what the souls are aware of.

QUESTION: What happens to the mind in the case of mental illness?

We could say, in general, that most mental illness is the manifestation of *fear*. The fear could either be: a *tendency* to fear that is placed by the soul into the human personality before birth; created by the personality itself during its human life; caused by inherent abnormal physiological structures that were intentionally implanted by the soul into the brain of the human body; or caused by certain physical disturbances in the brain that occur during the human life.

To illustrate the influence of the soul's choices, we would ask you to imagine a jar that is filled with peanut butter. And you would put a knife into it in order to dip out some peanut butter to eat. Then, a person would come after you and would say, "What happened to the peanut butter? It is no longer smooth. It has a chunk missing." Now, there were very important *purposes* that led up to that chunk being missing. Those purposes were related to your desire to eat peanut butter. But, let us say that the one who came after you is concerned with a pretty, smooth jar of peanut butter. They become very agitated, and they lament, "There is a chunk missing. The peanut butter is ruined. It is bad."

Here, you have a situation that is similar to one in which a soul would say, as it creates its human personality matrix: "There are some very important purposes for this new personality that I am creating to have *less* than a stable and normal mental functioning." Because of the soul's purposes, in the human personality there will be some "chunks" missing from its experience. There will be some gaps in its thinking. There will be some distortions. There will be a tendency for fear to dominate some of the thinking processes. From the soul's point of view, the mental imbalance is "good." It is meaningful. It is important to the purposes of the soul for the personality not to have ordinary mental functioning.

However, you as a relative of such a person, or the doctor of the person, would say, in effect, "I desire a smooth jar of peanut butter." You might say, "I do not desire to be with a human who is quite bizarre in their thinking, who might have violent tendencies, who interprets reality in a distorted way." You would say, "The mind of this one is wrong, bad, abnormal." And, from the human point of view, it is true that it is *abnormal*. But, it is not *bad*.

We would say that most mental illness that grows out of birth choices that have been made by the soul, or that simply emerges spontaneously in a person without any extraordinary trauma in the life of the one, can usually be considered to be *intended* manifestations that have been chosen by the soul for important reasons.

There are other areas of mental illness that are caused by the fear, pain, terror, or pressure of present human experience. In such cases, the fear of the human being has become so great that *they cannot stand their own negative thoughts and feelings.* Unconsciously, in terror, they "push a gap" through the normal mental energies, and they cause a kind of "break" in the rhythmic, harmonious balance of the energy patterns of ordinary thought. Sometimes they can repair the break. Sometimes not. The distortion of the thinking processes caused by the fear can be permanent or temporary, depending upon the individual, and, *depending upon the intensity of the fear in the ones around the individual.* But, in general, you could see such mental illness as a kind of forced break in the ordinary rhythms of thought, making it difficult for the individual to think in normal ways because of patterns of disconnected or distorted thinking.

QUESTION: There is a wide range between a genius and someone of low intelligence. Is the potential for high intelligence always there? Does activating that potential depend upon our present lifetime, or is the potential placed there by the soul before we are born?

First of all, human intelligence is an *energy* that is large and unlimited as it exists in the non-physical personality matrix mind that we described earlier. Therefore, the *potential* for intelligence in human beings is also un-limited, except for individuals with physical challenges to the brain. Usually, with brain injury, the physical brain is "squeezed," and there will be less intellectual functioning or capacity, less mirroring of the non-physical personality matrix mind.

Most souls of human beings, before the physical birth of the physical body, will choose what we might call an "average" intelligence, an average quickness to the mental capacities, and an average capacity to know and learn. And, most human beings will tend to not *fully* express that average capacity. So, many who appear not so intelligent have chosen average intelligence from birth, but, during their life, they have not paid enough attention to their thinking to stimulate it, and excite it, and cause it to become average intelligence.

Some souls will choose for the personality, either certain *limited* energies in the mind structure, or, they will infuse some blockages into the circulation of the blood that passes through the brain, or other physical areas, that will manifest as a mental *slowness*. Assuming that there is no brain damage, this will manifest as a personality who has less capacity for intellectual brilliance and intellectual activity. Such persons will not think as quickly, or as complexly. This kind of mental activity is *chosen* by the soul for particular purposes, and, unless the individuals make an extraordinary effort to stimulate the mind, they will generally function at that level of intelligence throughout the human lifetime.

In other souls, at the opposite end of the spectrum,

they will, for many reasons, choose as a purpose of the personality in this lifetime, *intellectual brilliance*. They will construct a mental configuration that is exceedingly intelligent, from the human point of view. However, as you ones in earth have observed, this does not always mean that the personality becomes an extraordinary individual. Sometimes, in those of intellectual brilliance, the *emotional* growth is not kept up.

In general, we could say that the *souls* will choose the general pattern of intelligence—whether average intelligence, high intelligence, or low intelligence. However, there will be a great deal of flexibility for the human beings, as they live their life, to make changes in the basic pattern. If one who feels they are of average intelligence wishes to use their intelligence more fully, then they will study, they will stimulate the mind, they will be active in thinking, questioning, and probing. They will learn to more fully use their mental capacities and increase their intelligence. One who does not wish to expand toward a fuller intellectual potential will tend to do the opposite— numbing themselves, narrowing their thinking, oversimplifying, overgeneralizing.

Within the range of potential intelligence, you can *choose* what to do with the choice made by your soul. You have freedom and flexibility. You can inadvertently *limit* your intelligence by not paying attention to your intellectual potential, or you can intentionally stimulate your potential and expand it toward the unlimitedness inherent in the *energies* of intelligence that are available to human beings.

QUESTION: Science tells us that we only use a small portion of our brain potential. Is that what you are talking about here?

We are speaking of the thinking capacities that are *reflected* by the brain. The fact that science has not yet delineated uses for all parts of the brain does not mean that those parts are not being used. As a general rule, the only lack of use of the brain in the present human race has to do with certain parts of the brain that are designated for *future* functions. Those areas have to do with *intuition*, and with psychic and spiritual perception.

This observation that you ones use only a small part of the brain is primarily due to the inability of science, as yet, to designate certain functions for certain brain areas. It then appears that those areas have no functions, or, that they are not being utilized. But, those areas of the brain play an important part in *creating the resonance necessary to reflect the personality matrix mind back to your human awareness.*

QUESTION: When a person is unconscious, or in a coma, what happens to the mind?

In general, the brain functioning is so muted that the ordinary brain "signals" that *reflect* the working of the non-physical mind are also muted. What you are used to as an ordinary input to your conscious awareness is simply cut off.

If you are in a coma, and your soul is intending for you to simply become conscious again—in other words, if you is it *not* intended by your soul that your physical body will die—then you will continue to live, so to speak, by the "rules" of the physical body. You will usually remain *blank* while you are unconscious. However, during this period of unconsciousness while you are in the coma, your *personality matrix* is not blank, or without awareness. It continues to be extremely active. But, since you have agreed to stay in the physical world and live by the rules of the physical brain, your *conscious* awareness will remain blank for as long as the coma may last. Yet, many important things will be happening between your personality matrix and your soul that you will not be consciously aware of.

If the coma is intended by your soul to lead to your physical *death*, then, most generally, your awareness will *not* continue to abide by the rules of physical life. You will gradually be stimulated to make some inner changes that will shift what was your ordinary human awareness *away* from your physical reality into a certain way of perceiving your eternal nature. So, even while your physical body is alive in a coma, your consciousness could be clearly and accurately aware of yourself as an eternal soul. At that point, you would have the option of looking down at your body in its coma in the physical world, and pondering the human beings who would be near your physical body, if you wished. But, if the unconsciousness is intended to last until your death, then, most likely, you would be finished with your body. You would simply abandon the body, realizing that you have much better things to do than to hover around an ended body that is no longer of any use to you.

QUESTION: It seems that many people's minds fail as they grow old. Is this an inevitability? All of us would like to remain mentally sharp until death. How can we best accomplish this?

Here we must generalize again, and we remind you that generalizations do not apply to all individuals. For most human beings, "senility" is *a lack of attention to outside stimulations.*

In general, unless there is a physiological breakdown of the body caused by putting harmful substances into the body, not giving enough attention to healthy food, exercise, rest, and so forth—assuming there is relatively sound physical health—then the loss of mental quickness and acuity is usually involved with a kind of *indrawing from the world.* This is a retreating into self-preoccupation, into smaller and smaller realms of thinking. There is a stifling of creativity, a smothering of curiosity, and a gradual shrinking, in terms of the use of the mind. This indrawing becomes a *habit,* which is self perpetuating.

Some human beings will become mentally inattentive because they simply are preparing for death, and their minds are no longer interested in the physical world. Others will become frightened, and they slowly begin to consciously or unconsciously shut off their feeling and thinking in order to avoid fears.

There are a number of reasons why the human mind becomes less active with old age, but the most generalizable one is: not participating enough in the world *outside* you; shrinking into your own narrow, self involved habits and allowing them to swallow you.

QUESTION: Earlier, you spoke of the part of the brain that will be activated in the future, that has to do with intuition, and perceiving the non-physical, spiritual dimensions of reality. Can we at this point amplify our perceptions of spiritual reality with our mind? If so, what is the best way to do this?

First of all, you would understand that, in general, the human race moves at a snail's pace through life. The evolutionary process will require many generations to take a step forward, particularly in the *physical* evolution. However, human mental and emotional evolution moves much more quickly.

At the present rate, in seven to twelve human generations from now, there would gradually begin to be human beings who would, at first, *be extremely sensitive to one another*, through love and harmony. Then, they would become sensitive to the eternal realities that animate life. Speaking in a general way, these ones who will open the areas of perception of spiritual realities will be ones who, through many lifetimes, have given themselves to a pursuit of truth. As human beings in past lifetimes, they have often desired to know more, to learn more, and to experience more.

If you would personally say, "I desire to accelerate this process in me now," and you are willing to dedicate yourself to the kind of work, and the patient, diligent experimenting that it takes, then your first need is to ask yourself, "What will I build this work upon?" What you will build upon is *your present human personality*. And, if your present personality is filled with fear, and doubt, and mistrust, then the work that you do will be filled with those qualities.

So, your first step in opening your perception of spiritual realities is: *working toward greater love and understanding of yourself and others, greater honesty with your fears and doubts, and greater courage to heal your negativity.* Those are areas that you will need to accomplish in order to fulfill yourself in this life, and they are the same areas that you will need to accomplish in order to accelerate this deepened, intuitive process within your personality.

Assuming that you are now working on these areas day by day, to the best of your ability, then you might say, "I wish to add a daily practice of disengaging from the limiting aspects of thinking and feeling that I have created, so that I may enter into a heightened, expanded, and intensified experience of my own mind, my own feelings." To accomplish this, you would set aside a period of silence each day. During that period of attunement, you would say to yourself:

> **"I am giving myself to the extraordinary forces of God that live inside me. And, in this moment, I ask that my thinking and my feeling be expanded in ways that will be beneficial to me, and to all those about me."**

This is the basic pattern for working with your thoughts and feelings. You would use this pattern in your own individual way. You would make periods of attunement each day, and you would direct yourself with these kinds of thoughts and feelings. During your attunement, you would practice opening your heart and your mind. Steadily, day after day, through such practice, you would begin to have results. And, if you continue to be balanced, and loving, and honest with your personality, and in your relationships with others, those results should enhance your experience of God, of your own soul, and of eternal realities.

This is a very general way to approach the expansion of your perceptions of spiritual reality. It requires intelligence, patience, and persistence. If you follow this way in an honest, loving manner, you will be quite pleased with the results that you attain.

For this moment, make a gentle relaxation, and imagine that you are using this method now. First, give yourself to love, and know that you are surrounded with love. Encourage in your own heart a feeling of wonderful love. Feel that you are being filled with love. And, as you do this, you can choose to say:

> **"I now give my mind into this extraordinary force of love. And I understand that *this force of love is God itself*. In this moment, I give my mind to God. And I ask that my mind be expanded, and opened, and stimulated in ways that will be beneficial to me, and to those about me."**

By doing this, you invite perfect growth and expansion, predicated upon the goodness of God itself, and not so much upon selfish desires.

For this moment, give yourself to this kind of thinking and feeling. And know that if you practice such an attunement in each day, you will expand your capacity to use your mind in ways that will bless you, and those about you, throughout this lifetime.

Chapter Three

ANGELS AND GUIDES

Inspiration From Beyond Earth

As you attempt to draw into your conscious mind, knowledge of beings who exist beyond the physical earth reality, you would need to ask of yourself a certain patience and tolerance. It would be as though you come to one without vision—one of blindness—and you say, "Now I shall teach you the *colors* of earth." Since the person cannot *see* the colors, in order to teach this person, you would have need, first of all, to create a way to communicate.

Since most ones on earth cannot see the beings who exist in the non-physical reality beyond earth, to help you learn about such beings, we will need to establish a way of communicating with you. To do this, from your side, you will need to begin by inwardly *loosening the rigidity of your ideas about life*—your conceptual structures—which are dominated by your present experience of *physical* reality. By loosening your present ideas about what is real in life, you will be able to expand your capacity to conceive of realities that lie beyond your present awareness.

As you inwardly become flexible in your thinking, from our side, we shall attempt to create for you, certain structures built with human words that can stimulate your intuitive capacities to sense and understand realities that, at present, lie beyond your currently manifested abilities to perceive. It is as though you are a cat, and you are trained to climb trees. We shall now attempt to spark in you, a latent ability to dig tunnels in the earth.

As a cat, you would not ordinarily be interested in digging tunnels. As a human being, you are trained to live in a *physical* world, and many of you are not ordinarily interested in exploring the areas of life beyond the physical. Most human beings are the cats happily climbing in the trees. For those who do desire to dig tunnels, we can be of service. We can help you augment your earth life with deep understandings of the beings who live in life without physical bodies. We can help you integrate this understanding into a physical life of love, wisdom, and knowledge of God itself.

Since you cannot directly perceive the realities that we shall attempt to show you, as we bring forth word structures to describe those realities, we ask that you realize that a portion of the understanding must come from yourself. There must be an inner, creative, imaginative response to the words we use. So, you would say to yourself, "My task is to take in these words and attempt to understand them in broader and deeper ways than such words in the past have been understood by me. I shall open a new frontier of understanding within myself, and, in so doing, I will begin to open my intuitive capacities to perceive realities that lie beyond the physical earth."

QUESTION: Would you give us a general overview of all of the kinds of non-physical beings?

If you would come to a zoo, and you would say, "Let us have an overview of all of the animals," you would most likely begin with *categories*. You might create categories for those animals who walk upon four legs, those who swim, those who fly, and so forth.

In attempting to make such groupings for you of the non-physical beings in life, we would need to begin with the understanding that such beings exist in a form that you would understand as *consciousness*. They are beings with a conscious awareness of themselves, and a conscious awareness of life, and they manifest, essentially, as *consciousness energy*.

To describe such beings, we would need to create categories, not according to physical form and shape, but according to *intensity of consciousness*. However, the idea of intensity of consciousness creates our first difficulty in communicating in human words. You are aware of such things as a range of intensity of *emotion*. If you have weak emotions you may feel flat. If you have very strong emotions, you feel more intense, fuller, more alive. But, it may be difficult for you to understand that in the range of consciousness, the *intensity* of consciousness determines, in essence, *a different being*. It is as if when you are having weak emotions you are one person, and when you are having very intense emotions, *you are an entirely different being*.

You must draw upon your own creativity and imagination as we use the limited words of earth to attempt to paint for you a picture of the way in which different intensities of consciousness manifest as the different non-physical beings of the universes. First of all, imagine a certain unlimited, undifferentiated force of consciousness that would stand, as it were, at the helm of the ship of life. You could understand this as the pure causative force that has created all life. It is an extraordinary force of love that could be considered to be the forces of the vastest expression of God. You might consider this to be the most *intense* energy of consciousness that exists.

From this *most* intense force, there radiates out energies of consciousness of great power that become personified as unique, individual consciousnesses, individual awarenesses. These become individual eternal beings. These beings are *less* intense consciousnesses than the causative force of life—the God forces. From your point of view, these individual awarenesses, or beings, are infinite in number.

Such eternal beings, in terms of *time* and *space*, were created with autonomous, independent, conscious awareness of themselves as living beings. And, from your point of view, they must be spoken of as beings with "energy" forms, since they have no *physical* shape or body, as you understand it.

All of these beings have begun a life that would be invisible to you, but to them it is quite real and tangible. And, in their lives, they have begun to orchestrate their own worlds. They do this with their own creativity, according to that which you would think of as *imagination*. But, each powerful imagining of these beings *becomes a tangible reality*. In essence, *each of their imaginings becomes a world unto itself.*

In a very simple way of speaking, we would say that infinite numbers of these "original beings" have created their own worlds, with forms, shapes, sounds, movements, and energies that are presently beyond your perceptions. Thus, in each of these beings, you have, as it were, a God—a creator of a world, or a universe.

Imagine then, that there is a being of this type who has created a world that eventually becomes what you now experience as your present *physical* universe. This being becomes the God of your world. This God is the *author* being of physical existence.

In this God, there is the capacity to send forth infinite numbers of forces similar to itself. These forces are unique, individual beings of a consciousness energy that is of less *intensity* than the God being. These beings would have self-awareness. You would understand them as your individual *souls*.

These souls, streaming forth from the God force, would be the means by which the God being would actually create the physical realities—stars, galaxies, and so forth—of your physical universe. The souls would create those realities in concert with your *author* being—the creator of the present universe, as you know it.

In a very complex way, the energy forms used for *physical* creation, are interwoven with energy forms used by all of the other infinite number of *author* beings, who are creating their own universes, which are *not* physical. This is an extraordinary weave of inter-penetrating energies, some physical, some non-physical.

These inter-penetrating energies are distinguished, or differentiated, by the *will* of each *author* being. According to the will of your *author* being, the complex energies have manifested in a weave of energy forms that has become, in your realm, *time* and *space*. In other realms, the energy weaves have become structures and concepts for which there are no human words.

Thus, you have a picture of an infinite number of *author* beings that, to your eyes, would be the Gods of all of life in all realms, physical and non-physical. They are distinguished by the *intensity* of their consciousness energy.

Now, let us focus upon your present physical universe. The *author* being of your world—and we remind you that this is a very simple way of expressing the consciousness energies that you would understand as God—would be the creator of all eternal souls having to do with human life, including your own soul. This *author* being has created you as an autonomous, conscious, self-aware, eternal soul. You as a soul are part of a large grouping of souls that have been involved in the creation of your present physical universe.

However, from that *author* being, there did stream forth other forms of life, or consciousness energy, that would be similar to your souls, but without the *rebellious* nature that you souls of earth did develop. These other beings you might consider to be, *angelic beings*. These angelic beings were willing to abide by certain patterns created by the *author* being, patterns that you might understand as *perfection*, or *love*. They were not interested in creating and penetrating the physical realm of form, of time and space. These angelic beings have chosen to continue to unfold a drama of beauty and magnificence in realities that are not physical, even though those realities are similar to the physical world in principles, in experiences, and in intensities of life.

The paths that you ones as souls involved with human expression have chosen to walk spring from the same causative source of love and creativity—the *most* intense consciousness energy of all creation—that set into motion all beings in all realms. Thus, you could say to yourself, "I am a portion of a vast network of loving beings who are unlimited in their creativity."

As a presently living human being, you have within your human self the same potent force of love, creativity, and unlimitedness that created all of life. So, to hold in your mind a simple understanding of the complexity of all of the beings of life, you can remember that these same qualities of love, creativity, and unlimitedness exist in all beings in all realms, even though the *forms* of their creations, the manner of their walking, and the nature of their path would be quite different than your own.

It is as though all ones come to speak to one another, each having their own unique voice, but all using the same language. Each is of the same consciousness energy of life, but some are of different intensities of that energy. Some speak with a soft voice, and some with a loud voice. All conscious, self-aware beings draw from the pure energy of life, an energy that you could understand as *love*. Each being then uses that energy in its own individual creativity and freedom of choice to manifest in the various realms of life. These realms of expression would, to your mind, be infinite.

QUESTION: Are all of these beings changing and evolving in some way? If so, how are they changing, and towards what are they evolving?

You could imagine that each of the energy structures in various realities that are similar to your structure of *time* and *space*, were set into motion by the first creative impulses of the *author* beings of that world, and that each world follows a kind of unfoldment that you could understand as *evolutionary change*. Quite simply put, you could see this unfoldment as the movement from seed, to plant, to fruit. This would appear to your vision as a process of growth that involves an expansion from a simple form to a more complex form.

It is as though you have a symphony. Each individual player in the orchestra plays the same piece of music, but with their own creativity. At first, they play in a simple way. Then, as they become more skilled and masterful, they play in a larger, fuller, more complex, and more evolved way.

All beings in all realms of life follow a certain similar principle of growth—they play the same music. They all follow an inner source of movement, or direction. Each world has an inner *thrust* or *impulse* which guides the unfoldment of that world within general outlines, or parameters. However, within the guidelines of each world, the beings within that world are free to create diversity, and they are limited only by the capacity to fulfill their potential for creativity. Thus, in essence, you would see all beings in all realms growing and changing in ways that are similar to your growth and change, but in most realms, the growth and changes are much more diversified and complex than in the present earth realm in which human beings express.

QUESTION: What is our place as human beings among all of these non-physical beings?

To help you to understand your capacity for integration with all of life through the various realms, we would ask that you imagine that you are a swimmer. You enter into the sea, by your own choice. You desire to swim. As you swim, you come upon a school of fish. You would ask, "What is my place amongst these fish?" Your place will depend upon the *choice* that you make in that moment, in relation to the fish. If you choose to observe the fish, then you are simply a visitor. If you are hungry and desire to catch them and eat them, then you are the destroyer of their realm.

Similarly, in a certain sense, your place amongst the many beings of life is determined by your human choice, and your creativity. In other words, you could be simply a small speck in life, if you choose to halt your evolutionary growth by a certain inward *death* of feeling. Then, the energy that is your present personality can become simply a dead "vehicle" that is absorbed by your soul as it continues its vast expansion through the present system of life that you know as your universe.

However, if your personality self chooses to consciously align with your soul, then there is a *sparking* of the energy form that you understand as your present human self. Through this, as a human being, you can become, in a certain sense, "eternalized." You can become the clear reflection of the soul force, and you set into motion your own process of creativity and evolution. In this sense, eventually, your place as a human being amongst other beings can become the place of a God, or a creator.

This is a complex area, for the place that you take among other beings, from the point of view of your present personality, will change according to the choices that you make in this lifetime. If you make certain choices of growth and love, your present personality can become an important part of your eternal being, which augments your eternal being in ways of great beauty. In that case, your human personality energy takes its place as a *creator*, just as all of your personalities of the past that have risen in love have taken their place as creator. Or, if you are unable to make such choices, if you become hopelessly lost in your own human distortion, your present personality energy can be dissolved into other areas of soul energy, and then re-fed into the soul, without that personality energy having a certain unique conscious awareness of itself. However, that personality energy is integrated into the higher conscious awareness of your own soul.

You could say that, as a human being, you relate to your soul as the child relates to the father. As you grow, you can become the father. As you become the father, you add to your soul, a new burst of energy, which then allows the soul to expand in different ways, in different worlds.

QUESTION: What are spiritual guides and what is their place in the structure that you have described?

The souls who choose to become guiding souls to human beings would be a portion of the grouping of souls that did choose to draw upon the God forces to create the physical universe that you now inhabit. These guiding souls, along with your own soul, and with other souls, in the beginning of time, did project their energies to create time and space, then to create the physical energies and forces that would later coalesce into planets, stars, and universes.

Then, these guiding souls would begin the *human* earth evolution with all of the souls who presently have human personalities living in physical form. These guiding souls would also project portions of themselves as personality energies into human bodies, through many lifetimes, just as your own soul has done, and is presently doing. However, the guiding souls, through many of their human personality lifetimes, would successfully pass through, and complete, the evolutionary stages of earth life, physically, mentally, and emotionally, until there would be a total mastery, in love, of all of earth life.

Then, you would see these guiding souls choosing *not* to enter any further into physical form, but taking upon themselves forms more closely aligned with the true nature of the *author* being, the God force. In essence, the guiding souls would become totally one with their own eternal nature, without any distracting impulses pulling them toward earth life. In this expanded form, they would use their soul forces as a vehicle to build, in spiritual realms, expansions of all of the magnificence that they, in human form, had created in earth life. In a very simple way of speaking, these guiding souls would begin to create *their own worlds* in eternal realities, as an extension of the magnificence they had created in human form.

Then, the guiding souls would align themselves with other beings who had also completed the human evolution, and who would also have a capacity to create their own worlds in spiritual realities. These spiritual worlds would be separate from the human, physical world. The beings creating these worlds would be free to choose to focus *only* upon their own realities and cease to occupy with the human expression. However, because of their love for human life, and for presently living human beings, these "advanced" souls, through their creative power, would act to "maintain contact" with human reality. They would initiate creations that would make it possible for them to serve as guiding souls to human beings.

To accomplish this, they would need to create a world that stands *between* their own *non*-physical spiritual worlds that are "distant" from human reality, and the human experience, which involves *physical* reality. This would be a "transition" world, in which we, as spiritual guiding ones, are able to perceive earth realities, to a certain extent. In this merging, we most certainly are able to share the deeper energies of you ones who walk in the physical earth.

You would understand that we maintain a certain "coexistence" between our world and yours. We would continue authoring our own worlds—advancing them through the expansion of love and creativity—and, at the same time, as it were, holding a "vision" of yourselves, penetrating your personal lives, and inwardly living with you moment by moment.

All human beings have past relationships established with their guiding souls, and all human beings have inner energies that in the present join them to their guiding souls, and to the transition world. However, most humans are unable to *consciously* enter into the deeper dimensions of reality of the transition world, so they are not consciously aware of their guiding souls. So, most human beings are guided in the *unconscious* portions of their human personality. It is the rare human, in this time, who walks with abilities to continually align with their guiding ones in a conscious way. Yet, we assure you that all human beings are intimately and deeply guided within themselves, even though they may not be aware of such guidance.

QUESTION: Would you talk to us about angels? What are angels?

To help you see this area more clearly, we would ask that you imagine that you have a moth flying in your room. And you would say, "That is a *buzzard*." Then, all of your children would call a moth a buzzard. And all of their children would call a moth a buzzard. In time, all ones would call a moth a buzzard. If one would ask you, "What is a buzzard?" you would describe a *moth*.

Now, as long as you do not realize what you have done, you believe that you are perceiving *truth*. So it was in the earlier stages of human life, particularly in the Christian tradition. As human beings tried to understand and describe the eternal forces of life, as those forces interacted with human existence, the human beings would give certain names and descriptions to their *experiences* of those eternal forces. However, those human descriptions did not always clearly reflect the *reality* of the eternal forces.

We remind you that in ancient human periods, the human personality interest in the *physical* world was very feeble. The human passion was for *eternal* realities. Human beings had a clear sense of *belonging* to eternal realities, not to the earth. And they had rather clear perceptions of their souls, and the eternal forces of God that constantly *create* the physical reality, out of an eternal fabric, or ground, or energy.

Woven into the very fabric of physical objects, bodies, planets, stars, and so forth, and sustaining space and time, there are, to put it crudely, "swirling forces," for which you have no name. We would need to call these forces, *energies*, but this word is too weak to convey the full truth of these magnificent eternal forces. It is as though you are embraced by the most beloved person in your life, and you feel an extraordinary feeling of love, and you would say, "This is an energy." You would under describe the reality. These swirling eternal forces would be extraordinary forces of goodness, love, creativity, joy, and many other wonderful things for which you have no words. So, to call them *energies* is to under describe the realities. These swirling energies would be expressions of the *author* being, the God forces, and the eternal souls.

In the early stages of human existence, the human personality structure lived on the physical earth in a *non*-physical body. You could imagine it as an *energy* body. At that point in human evolution, the magnificent swirling eternal energies of life were perfectly perceived, or almost perfectly perceived, by human beings. And these eternal energies were understood for what they were—which you would presently understand as the forces of God.

In ancient periods, after human beings had lived for a while in the tangible, physical bodies that are similar to present bodies, the swirling eternal energies were *vaguely* perceived by human beings. There was a kind of "veil" over the human vision of eternal realities. Since human beings could not clearly perceive and *experience* the eternal forces within their inner life, they began to *name* those realities, and *describe* them, so that they could communicate about them in human language in the outer world. This began the human distortion of eternal realities. If the eternal forces are a moth, then human beings, not clearly perceiving the moth, began to call it a buzzard.

Now, it does not matter what word you use to describe eternal forces and beings. It matters *how you perceive those eternal realities*, from your point of view. In other words, in the *larger* view of reality, it does not matter so much what anything is in life, for it is *all* growing out of the same eternal fabric of God, and life. However, from your human point of view, it matters a great deal. You have many discrete forms and realities in your earth life, and you wish to keep them straight, so that you can understand them, and manipulate them. So, human beings must *name* the various manifestations of life, and you must experience them as being different from one another.

In the earlier stages of human life, when human beings were living in the solid physical bodies, and there was the veil over their perception of spiritual realities, for certain eternal beings that they vaguely perceived, they would create a *name*. That name would *not* be the present word, *angel*. It would be a name for which there is now no surviving word. It was a name that meant, essentially, *the emanations from the divine God-source,* meaning the magnificent, swirling eternal energies that we have described that permeate and sustain physical reality.

In the beginning of human understanding, this word, in various languages, would always mean, *the emanations from the divine God-source.* However, in time, there would come about variations in the name.

As humans began to make writings in ancient periods, and particularly in the ancient Hebrew tradition, the writings would begin as a genuine attempt to capture, in words, the reality of the human experience of the swirling forces of God. But, gradually, the writings would be overseen by ones of tribal leadership, and, eventually, religious groupings. Then, in various writings, overseen by these human leaders with specific purposes of their own, it became very important what the *words* meant, and there was little concern for the *reality* that the words were supposed to describe.

So, the ancient word that meant, *the emanations from the divine God-source*, was passed along through many generations, and many languages, until it came to be the present word, *angel*. The word angel is primarily an expression of the need of human beings to make tangible, in a form that represents idealism, the magnificent forces of eternal reality. The word is necessary because the capacity to *directly experience* God was gradually lost. Thus, human beings needed to *think* about God and eternal realities. So, the concept of *angel* was created, as a representation of the swirling, divine forces. However, under the influence of human motives, an angel would become a human-like creature of idealistic and perfect quality.

Since it is so difficult for human beings to penetrate the actual *reality* referred to with the word, *angel*, there is a certain benefit to having that word to use. For your own use, you could say that an angel is a swirling, divine being with perfect qualities. If you wish to put wings on it, that can be quite entertaining for you. You can put horns on it, or hooves, or anything that pleases you. Simply know that in so doing, you are working with human symbolism—words and ideas—and not with *truth*.

The most important aspect of the concept of angel is *perfection*—perfect love, perfect understanding, perfect beauty, perfect goodness. So, it is beneficial to use the world angel to represent such perfection.

QUESTION: Are angels the same as spiritual guides? If not, how are they different from our guides?

Human beings need to feel a *personal* connection to spiritual realities. And, in the representation of angelic beings as guardians, or guides, human beings are trying to make the swirling divine forces of life more personal. However, in this, there is some confusion.

In the strictest sense, the swirling divine forces are the moth. The word *angel* refers to the buzzard. In other words, the swirling divine forces that you call angels, although they penetrate all of physical reality—and here the human words are very difficult to use—we must say that the swirling forces are not "personal." This does not mean that they are *impersonal*. They are extraordinary forces of love, but, they have to do with *all* of earth reality—all humanity, all physical matter.

There are other swirling divine forces that you could accurately call *beings*, or *souls*, that you might consider to be a bit more *focused*, more specialized, and more "personal" than angels. Your own soul would be one of these beings. The guiding souls to human beings are also beings who are of a more personal nature. These guiding souls are the souls who have completed their human evolution, and who have chosen to express in the transition world in which they serve as guiding souls to human beings.

So, in the strictest sense, guiding souls would be different than the realities that have been symbolized as angels. However, gradually, the human understanding of *angel* is coming closer to a description of a guiding soul, particularly when you think in terms of a "guardian angel." But, in ancient times, angel was closer to the not-personal swirling divine forces that we have described.

What is important here is not so much whether you accurately capture the spiritual reality in your intellectual understandings, but whether your understandings bring *benefit* into your present human life. So, whether it is precisely accurate or not, it is more important and beneficial to you to see angelic beings as personal, beloved, perfect beings who guide you, than to see them, in a more abstract way, as swirling energies that sustain physical matter.

QUESTION: What is a fallen angel? Is that a human concept?

Here, again, there are simply no human words for some of the areas that we must look at to bring clarity for you. So, we must use the words that come closest to the *feelings* of the realities that we are trying to show you.

In a certain way, the forces of God that have to do with

physical matter—forces that take the form of what we have described as the angelic forces that swirl through matter—in their *normal* energy structures, or configurations, could be said to be, in human words, of a very fast "vibration rate." Certain portions of these forces in the beginning of the creation of physical reality needed to "slow their vibration rate" as they created and sustained physical matter. So, there was a kind of "making tangible" of their energies. These beings did not become concrete, or solid, or physical, but the energies of these beings became "thicker," or denser.

In the early stages of human existence, a human being with enlightened vision could see a "gradation" of the energies of these swirling angelic forces. At one end of this spectrum of energies, the human being would see the extraordinary swirling energies that did *not* have to do with physical matter. The vibration rate of these energies would appear very "fast." The energies would seem refined, and rarefied. At the other end of the spectrum, the human being would see the angelic forces of beings involved in sustaining physical matter. These energies would have a "slower" vibration rate. Thus, the human being would perceive the energies as heavier, denser.

Because of this difference in perception, in the communication between early human beings, there would be a distinction made between the *rarefied* angelic energies, and the *heavy*, *dense* angelic energies. In the beginning, this would not be a *pejorative* distinction. The human beings might speak of a "light angel" and a "dark angel," simply as a distinction between two different perceptions.

Over a period of time, as human beings began to create fear and negativity, many complex changes took place in the human understanding of life. There came into being *contrasts*, or *opposites*. Opposites are not a reality of life. They are a *human created concept*.

The human created opposites that came about in human evolution created a belief in *good* and *bad*, morally speaking. So, the distinction that early human beings made between the *refined* angelic energies and the *heavy* energies—the light angels and the dark angels—was gradually distorted to become *good* angels and *bad* angels. Then, when there came the writing down of religious beliefs and traditions, propagated by the human-created churches, the human ideas of good and bad led to the belief that the "bad" angels were *fallen* angels. Thus, you can see that, in reality, there are no fallen angels. This is a concept, created by human beings.

QUESTION: What is the relationship between human beings, spiritual guides, angels, and God?

The intuitive groping of past human societies toward a deification of life, or the symbolizing of life in a form of God, is an intuitive response to the force within each human being that you would consider as God itself. This can lead you to understand God, from your present point of view, in terms of various "levels" of existence.

As we have pointed out, the "largest" level of existence would be considered to be the God of all of life, or the creative force of all beginning causative effects. In the ultimate sense, this God is the *author* of all consciousness.

The next level of existence would be the infinite number of *author* beings that we have described as "streaming forth" from this God force. These beings create the *forms* in which consciousness expresses in many realms of life, physical and not physical.

For simplicity, you could think of one of these *author* beings as the author of the next level of existence, which includes all of the souls who are involved in the present physical universe. It would be appropriate to include "angels" in this grouping of souls who were created by the author being, and who are involved in physical reality. You could see the souls of this level as ones who help maintain physical creations, but who do *not* choose to manifest portions of themselves in *human* form.

The souls of your present human personalities would be the next level of existence. Your own soul would be one of these souls. And, we remind you that *you* are that soul. You could also include here the souls who have completed their human evolution, and who now express as spiritual guides to human beings.

The next level of existence would be the human personality structure of energies—the *personality matrix*—as it exists *apart* from your physical body. This Includes your *conscious awareness of yourself* as a projection of your own soul, but also many unconscious energies that pour into your personality matrix.

The next level of existence would be the human experience *inside* of a physical body. This would be yourself as you consciously experience yourself on earth in this moment.

In time, you will understand this complexity in a clearer way. For the present, we suggest that you hold in your mind, and in your feelings, these simple structures that we have given. And, in each day you can say the truth to yourself in this way:

> **"The true relationship between God, angels, guiding souls, my soul, myself as a human being, and all of life in all realms, is maintained by an extraordinary energy of *love* that unites all of life. In our essence, we are all the same. We differ only in our *manifestations* as this love energy is funneled through the creativity and free will of all of the beings of life."**

This can be an inspiring and beneficial way to encourage your thoughts and feelings to more closely align with the spiritual realities that you cannot now directly perceive.

QUESTION: What is the purpose of spiritual guides, and does every human being have their own guide or guides?

As we have pointed out, many souls have mastered earth to such an extent that they no longer desire to project a portion of themselves into human form. They have begun to create their own non-physical worlds. However, their love for human life prompts them to offer themselves as guiding souls for presently living human beings. As we have described, they have created a non-physical "transition world" between their world and the world of human life on earth. By entering this transition world, they can align with, and communicate with human beings.

In this transition world, there is a constant kind of "communication" between the guiding souls and the souls of human beings living on earth. So, when your own soul created your present personality, preparing to project that personality forth into your physical body at your birth, your soul did communicate with various guiding souls. The guiding souls could see, with their great loving hearts, the fear, pain, and suffering that you had created in your *past* human lifetimes on earth. They desired to help you heal that negativity. They also desired to be a force of inspiration and guidance for you while you walk upon the earth in a physical body. Therefore, in their love, they voluntarily agreed to come forth to walk into the transition world, between their life and the earth life of your new human personality, to serve as your guiding souls.

Thus, you could say that the purpose of your spiritual guides is to help you manifest the fullness of your being in your present lifetime by filling you with their love and their inspiration. They also attempt to inspire you to draw upon your full abilities to heal human fear and negativity, the cause of all of your past pain.

The purpose of your guiding souls is *not* to make your life choices for you. It is *your* purpose to choose how you will live your life, and to choose what to think, feel, and *do* day by day throughout your life.

All human beings living on earth have guiding souls. The individual soul of each human being will guide the human personality that it creates, but, also, several guiding souls will come forth to help provide inspiration, guidance, and love to that human being.

QUESTION: How do spiritual guides actually guide us in our daily lives?

This is a very important area for you ones who seek conscious knowledge of your guiding ones. First of all, we assure you that the guiding souls to yourself guide you through inner forces and processes that *can never be disrupted.*

In a manner that involves very complex energy interactions, your guiding souls guide you through the very cells of your physical body. They "speak" to those cells through an energy of perfect *stimulation* and *growth.* To accomplish this, your guiding souls weave *their* energy with the force that you would understand as the creative God force that flows through your soul to your present personality, and the creative God force that flows from certain *author* beings who have to do with your human life. Your guiding souls mingle their influences upon you with the many influences of God that enter into you as *a stream of life.*

However, your guiding souls have a capacity to enter "deeper" into your human existence. They can come into that area which is the personal, intimate aspect of your human personality structure. This area is the small, temporary sphere of private creativity which is your day to day, moment to moment, awareness of life. This is also your self awareness—your private experience of being aware that you are you.

Even though, in your *unconscious* life, you are *always* being fed by energies of the perfection of God, from all of its areas of manifestation, you can create a shell about your private center and refuse to become *consciously* aware of truth, of love, of the real nature of life. And, temporarily, nothing can enter into that shell except your own soul and your guiding souls. This is quite simplified, but it can give you a base of understanding.

Your guiding souls enter into your private center through what you could call, for lack of larger earth words, "subliminal forces." These subliminal forces can possibly affect your conscious awareness, but you usually do not notice them. Thus, even though the energy of your guiding souls comes *closer* to your conscious awareness than do the deep, unconscious energies of God that feed you, the energies of your guiding souls are still within your *unconscious* life. The other God forces also speak to you in an unconscious way. All of these energies will flow into your unconscious life, no matter what you choose in your life. But, to go further and receive *conscious* guidance, you will need to exercise your *choice*.

You must consciously *choose* to become aware of the influence of your guiding souls. Your guiding souls will work with you throughout your lifetime, but, if you do not choose to work toward conscious awareness of them, they will work with you in an unconscious way. You must choose to invite the energies of your guiding souls through your *threshold of conscious awareness*.

If you choose to *think* about your guiding souls each

day, to work toward *love* for them, to inwardly *sensitize* yourself to their existence, then you can eventually bring your connectedness to your guiding souls into your conscious awareness. As this occurs, your guiding souls can begin to work through your thoughts, and through your emotions.

Your guiding souls will usually influence your *ordinary* thoughts and emotions. Such an influence will usually feel like a deep inspiration, and clarity, but, it will perhaps feel like *you*. It is quite rare that guiding souls will work in *tangible* ways, such as in those human beings who would hear words apart from their own thinking, or see physical visions of their guiding souls. For most ones of earth, the guiding souls will work through your thoughts and your emotions to inspire you to choose to refine those thoughts and feelings with love, patience, honesty, nobility, idealism, and honor.

QUESTION: Can we ask for help from the angelic forces that you have described? If so, how is this different from asking our spiritual guides for help?

First of all, you would say that your ''job'' in this lifetime is to be as fully *human* as possible. However, there is a greater human fullness that is possible when you have a passion for the *divine*—for God, for love, for truth, for idealism. Such a focus actually *expands* your human experience. So, if, of your own free will, you *choose* to align your responsibility to live fully as a human being with a passion for truth, and for God, you will open the way to great benefit for yourself, and for humanity.

However, what is important in this is the *inner experience of God*, not the *vision* of God, the *sound* of God, the *smell* of God, the *touch* of God, or the *taste* of God. Those are the human senses of the *physical body*. The forces of God are *not* physical realities, although they underlie and sustain physical matter.

As a human being, you are not perceptually equipped to directly perceive the forces of God in their naked forms, for they are not physical forms. While you are in your physical body, it is simply impossible for you to *directly* perceive God in its fullness. You have agreed to this as a condition of your human existence. What this means is that while you are in your present human form, you will not *directly* perceive God in its own forms. You will not *directly* perceive angelic forces in their true form. You will not *directly* perceive your own soul, or your guiding souls in their true form.

Thus, for these realities, since you cannot directly perceive their true non-physical forms, you will need to *create* forms for them—forms that you *can* perceive. You will need to translate the spiritual, non-physical forms into something that you can be consciously aware of in your own life in the physical world.

You can translate these forms *unconsciously*, by being manipulated by your present beliefs, or by teachings given to you by others, or even by your own fears and doubts. Or, you can consciously *choose* to use forms that serve you best in your life. For example, if the form of an *angel* feels very negative to you, for whatever reasons, you would *not* choose to translate the swirling divine forces that sustain life into the form of a *concept*, *idea*, or *image* of an angel. If a *donkey* is a form that inspires love in you, you would benefit more by translating the divine forces into a donkey. You would say that there are donkeys that swirl about in life, projected forth by God to sustain physical reality.

It does not matter what form you choose for the spiritual realities that you cannot perceive, as long as the form you choose opens your heart, and helps you feel the truth of the spiritual realities. The clearest way for you to perceive God and truth in your lifetime as a human being is through your *feelings*, not through your vision or your other physical senses. Not even through your thoughts.

So, you could say to yourself each day:

"I am guided by souls from beyond human life who penetrate me constantly within my personality structure as a human being. I cannot perceive the form of these guiding souls, so I will *create* a form that stirs my heart."

If the image of an angel touches you most, then your guiding souls are angels, and when you are asking for help, you will attune to angels. If the image of a butterfly touches you most, then your guiding souls are butterflies, and you will ask butterflies for help.

This is an *emotional* issue, so you can test, with your feelings, the various images available to you. If necessary, you can create new images that have never existed before. Test them all to see how they make your feel. With the images that touch you most deeply, use them.

When they no longer touch you, then create new ones. It is not the image of the form that is important. It is the feeling associated with the image.

You are searching for images and forms that stir in you a feeling that you are deeply loved, that you are closely guided, and that you are celebrated by God and eternal souls. Create the forms that stir such feelings, use them each day, and rejoice in them.

QUESTION: Are all spiritual guides the same kind of beings?

For your purposes, it is beneficial to assume that all guiding souls to all human beings in earth are the same kinds of beings that we have described for you.

QUESTION: Are there different levels from which spiritual guides guide us?

In the human personality, particularly in this present period of the strong influence of *science*, there is a human fondness for thinking in terms of unfolding cycles of growth, and the progressive building of life, one stage upon the other. You ones are quite attracted to concepts of *levels* and *stages*. And, the nature of eternal reality is so complex and foreign to human functioning that the closest you ones can come to grasping it at this time is through the use of your concepts of levels and stages. However, the challenge here is that even though these concepts are the most effective for human beings to use to think about the non-physical realities of life, the truth is that beyond human existence, there are *no* levels or stages.

Beyond earth life, and indeed, penetrating the energies of earth life, there are interlocking, ever expanding waves and cycles of "energies," manifesting as *realms of experience* of beings who are rooted in an eternal unlimitedness and magnificence, for which there are no human words. Yet, to speak of the spiritual guidance that you receive as a human being, we will need to speak of levels and stages as the only way to communicate that which cannot be communicated. Simply remember that the *reality* is quite different than these concepts of levels and stages.

As we have mentioned, there are forces of your soul and your guiding souls that are continually being fed into the unconscious portions of your human personality. At this unconscious "level," all of these energies of spiritual guidance function perfectly. At this level, you are being *fully* penetrated by eternal energies. You would need to understand these energies as *magnificence, total wisdom,* and *love*. This occurs at the deepest level of your personality existence.

At the next level "above" this, moving toward your conscious awareness, there is a level of experience that is the level of your *humanity*. It is the *individualizing* factor that makes you a unique human being. This makes you *yourself*. This is your present *human self awareness*, which is one "sliver" of your soul awareness that has been projected into your personality matrix of energies.

This level of your humanness could be said to have some levels within it. At the deepest level of you humanness, your experience would be *unconscious*. This level mingles with the more deeply unconscious level at which you are being fully penetrated by spiritual energies.

At this deepest level of your humanness, your patterns are essentially uninfluenced by any human distortion that you might create in your conscious thoughts or feelings. Thus, if you can learn to enter this deep level of consciousness through a thorough, steady, and honest inner attunement, then the spiritual guidance that you receive in your conscious mind and feelings will be closer to the truth of what your guiding souls are attempting to make you aware of. You could say, ''I am receiving spiritual guidance from the deepest level that I can bring into my *conscious* awareness as a human being.''

If you would go any ''deeper'' than this level, you would ''lose'' yourself as a human being. There would no longer be a discreet human personality, and you would stand as an eternal soul.

The level above this deepest level of your humanness could be considered to be, the ''ninth degree of attainment.'' We use these words simply to mean that if you consciously attune to this level, ninety percent of your self created human negativity will be *absent*. If you attune to spiritual guidance at this level, only ten percent of your human negativity will distort the truth.

With this very crude structure, you could imagine that the next level of attunement is the ''eighth degree of attainment,'' where only eighty percent of your negativity will be absent, and twenty percent will distort the guidance. This image of levels would continue on toward your conscious awareness—seventy percent, sixty percent, fifty percent, and so forth—until you come to your ordinary, day to day conscious awareness as a human being, in which one hundred percent of your human distortion is present. This means, essentially, that zero percent of clear, true spiritual guidance can reach your *conscious* awareness. At this level, the spiritual guidance can still be consciously perceived by you, but it will be mingled with one hundred percent of your human fears, doubts, confusions, and misunderstandings about life.

Now, you must not assume that your ordinary, conscious level of existence, at which your distortions are fully present, is *inferior* to the deeper levels of consciousness. You need to rejoice in your ordinary experience, and celebrate your day to day conscious life. Indeed, many ones at this time would be much happier if they would seek spiritual guidance from their "ordinary" level of awareness, for, often, their search for deeper, "purer" guidance will cause them to become critical of their ordinary personality experience. They will begin to distrust themselves and their own ability to make important choices in life. The "ordinary" part of you needs to be appreciated, encouraged, and loved.

So, in terms of *levels* from which you receive spiritual guidance, you could assume that the influences of love and inspiration from your guiding souls always comes from the same magnificence of eternal realities—from the same "level." or reality The difference in the clarity of guidance you perceive as a human being is determined by the level of consciousness within your personality that you attune to in any moment.

QUESTION: Are there any *negative* entities that can influence us as we try to attune to our guiding souls?

We can assure you that in all of the realms of reality, there are no negative beings. Negative beings are created by the brilliant, and unlimited capacity of human beings to *imagine*.

You must be aware that your imagining does not stop inside your private *inner* experience. It can extend to the *outer* world through your physical organs of perception—your ability to see, hear, touch, taste, and smell. Thus, in certain ways, and under certain circumstances, you have the capacity to literally project before your own physical eyes, ears, and so forth, three dimensional visions of the negativity that you have created inside yourself through your imagination.

There are some human beings who believe that they have seen "demonic" personages in "solid" form. Some have even been convinced that they have been "possessed" by these personages. We can promise you that such experiences are created by their human imagination, saturated with fear and misunderstanding.

Since your imagination can be so powerful, if you desire to make a deep attunement to your guiding souls, and you believe that their are negative entities in life, then it is wise to heal your fears, and discover the confusion in your beliefs, before you make your deep attunement. For, it is possible for you to, unconsciously, and unintentionally, harness the power of God that lives within you, feed it into your imagination, saturate it with fear, and create for yourself what seems to you to be a real experience of negative entities.

If you did this, it would not change the *nature* of the magnificent forces that you are drawing upon. They would still be ''positive'' beings. Yet, even though you are drawing upon positive energies, your unintentional creation of the illusion of negative beings could be temporarily frightening and painful for you.

For those who are willing to believe that *all negativity and ''badness'' in life lives in human thought, feeling, imagination, experience, and action*, there can be a positive, joyful attunement to your guiding souls. If you create fears, you will heal them, knowing that they live inside your human personality. As you heal your own fears, you will come to realize that if human beings heal their self created negativity, then you can say that, in truth, there is only *goodness* in life.

QUESTION: Would you tell us how we choose our guides before we come into earth?

Imagine yourself as one who is coming into a large banquet hall in the sky. Perhaps you would speak of this as *heaven*. Imagine this as the reality before you come into your present body.

In this place, you are the *soul* of yourself. You are also the many human personalities that you have created for your past earth lifetimes. Now, you are preparing to project a portion of your soul awareness into a new personality matrix of energies that will soon enter a physical body that will become you, as a human being.

In your preparations, you begin to look about the heavenly banquet hall to choose the souls who will become the guiding soles for your new personality. In much the same way as you might search for a mating one on earth as a human being, you look first for forces of *attraction*.

There are many souls available, for you have a deep love relationship to each one in the banquet hall. In other words, the forces of God align you with all possible guiding souls. However, some guiding souls express the uniqueness of that which you would consider to be a kind of "personality" attraction. Some attract you more than others.

The guiding souls stand in a certain, as it were, calm perfection, loving all ones totally. So, they are not so much *attracted* to you, for they would love you regardless of your choice. They would rejoice in you whether you would choose them as guiding ones or not. The attraction is primarily from yourself, as a personality/soul combination who is preparing to invest your new personality in the physical fetus form that will eventually become your present body.

You begin, then, to pull yourself toward certain guiding souls through your *attraction*. These attraction energies are quite complex, but you could speak of them simply as personality *likes* and *dislikes*, even though in this realm there would be no negativity. In essence, you are attracted by a brilliance, a radiance, that mirrors your ideal most perfectly. This sparks a creativity between yourself and the guiding souls who are capable of personifying all of the ideals that will satisfy the needs that your new personality will have.

There would also be many past connections between yourself and the guiding souls that you are attracted to. Some of these connections would be established when those guiding souls did walk as a human being in past times with you, sharing human relationships of love with your past personalities.

Eventually, you would choose several guiding souls who would work within your human personality throughout your new lifetime. Before your human birth, working as your own soul, in harmony with the guiding souls that you have chosen, and with other beings, you would establish a general, loose life plan for your new personality. This would be a kind of "script" for the human drama that you will play out. However, it would simply be a loose "sketch," to be refined by your personality as it makes it choices throughout the lifetime.

QUESTION: Since most people are not consciously aware of spiritual guides, what tangible evidence can we find that these guides exist?

First of all, you would say, "If I could *believe* enough, I could find evidence in my toenails, for I could look at them and feel a merging between my body, my personality, my soul, my guiding ones, and all that is." *Without* belief, it will be quite difficult to find any evidence at all, for each of you has agreed to abide, as it were, by the "rules" of earth, and these rules are quite important to you.

Therefore, this is a matter of *belief*. And this flies in the face of your present training, whereby you would say,

"Give to me the proof and I agree to believe." In a certain way, you must say, "I agree to believe in order to find proof."

The first step, then, for finding tangible evidence of guiding souls in your life is to entertain the belief that such evidence already exists. You must assume that you have simply overlooked it. You would need to say, "Given my present life, without needing to change it, where could I find evidence of guiding ones, if I believe that they do exist?"

You could start with the *inspiration* in life. When you are sitting in despair, and there comes a telephone call, and it is a friend who would say, "I had an impulse to call you," then, if you have *belief*, you can say, "Here my guiding ones have inspired my friend to call me, knowing that I am in need of tangible assistance in my despair."

In a more dramatic way, imagine that you lie in a hospital bed, quite ill. Your lungs are filled with infection. You cannot breathe. You begin to despair. Death is very near. Then, quite abruptly, there comes a certain brilliant thought into your mind. Perhaps the thought might be: "God walks with me, and I now ask God to heal me and give me further time on earth." If there is belief in you, you could say that the thought to ask for help from a higher power was implanted in you by your guiding ones, for you had so infested your thoughts with negativity, that it would not have occurred to you to ask for powers from beyond earth. That spark, to remind your mental capacity to ask for help, you could *choose* to see as evidence of your guiding souls.

Once you have begun to believe, evidence of guiding souls abounds. If you would not even be willing to entertain the belief, most likely, you could walk an entire lifetime with no evidence, creating the feeling of walking alone, creating feelings of isolation and abandonment.

QUESTION: Many people have difficulty imagining the non-physical world of spiritual guides. What is the nature of their existence?

In this area, you have entered a realm that is much like entering a cave where there is no light at all. You desire to know the nature of the darkness in the cave. So, you light a torch. Immediately, the darkness is gone. You cannot study the darkness, for it is overshadowed by the light from your world.

This is the challenge that we face in attempting to help you conceive of our realm of existence as guiding souls. As soon as we create words about ourselves to reflect ourselves to you, we become a product of the words. You perceive the words, and their human meanings, but your present mind does not posses the perceptive capacity to capture our essence. Your perception of our existence is overshadowed by the very words that we must use to describe that existence.

It is as though you desire to taste the juice of the orange, but your mouth has been sealed shut. Perhaps, as a crude substitute, you could put the orange in your nose, but still, you have not truly tasted. As a crude substitute then, as it were, to put our oranges in your nose, we will attempt to make words that, even though they are not truly reflective of ourselves, at least will point out a direction for your own thoughts and your own intuitive sensing.

Imagine that you stand in a desert. You hold grains of sand in your hand. One grain of sand represents that which you presently know about yourself and life—your whole experience as a human being. Then imagine that your mind says, "These thousands of miles of desert are composed of the same sand as the one grain that represents my knowledge, therefore, all of these grains of sand are the same, therefore I know them all." If you look at a large desert, it is not the same as looking at one grain of sand. Yet, in a certain way, the desert is only one grain of sand, multiplied infinitely.

If you would imagine all of the idealism, beauty, love, power, and creativity that you can possibly conceive of in your present moment, and apply it to yourself, this would be one grain of sand. Then, imagine that the realm of existence of guiding souls is the desert. It would be the idealism, beauty, love, power, and creativity magnified to such a degree that it goes beyond your limits of imagination. As you *feel* this image that represents the love that permeates the spiritual realms, then you are coming nearer to the experience of your own soul, of guiding souls, of that which you would speak of as God.

You could say that guiding souls exist in qualities of experience that, quite unsatisfactorily, would need to be called *feelings*. We exist also in forms that have to do with *motion*, as you would understanding it—movement—

circumscribed by *choices*. In other words, we have the choice to be unlimited, to merge with "all that is." At the same time, we have the freedom to circumscribe ourselves, to create certain temporary limits so that the *intensity* of our experience can be *focused* in certain ways. This focus is remotely associated with *form*, as you would understand it.

All of this can be quite confusing to follow in words. This an area that you must penetrate through your *imagination*, for the words cannot contain it. Imagine that we exist in forms that would be symbolized by that which many have attempted to speak of as God. Say to yourself then, "My guiding ones represent *perfection*, as I can conceive it. They live in a realm that would be similar to my experience of myself as a *total* being, not only a physical being, but including my imagination, my dreams, my ideals, the unlimited scope of my mind and my feelings. They exist in a world similar to this, but magnified many fold. I can symbolize them as similar to human ones, but of total perfection."

QUESTION: You have mentioned that spiritual guides have been physical human beings in the past. Do guides ever appear in physical form to us now?

When you align your personality thoughts, emotions, and beliefs in certain ways that, in the past, you have done in religious groupings or in mystical orders, you open a door to your soul, and you realign with ancient capacities to master the very molecules of the earth itself. You ones, in your *soul* forms, in the beginning of time, did *create* those molecules. You did then align them into the physical substances of matter that you now you live within as human beings.

Throughout the history of mankind, certain human beings have temporarily created moments in time in which they could project their beliefs so powerfully into the earth forces that they could arrange for there to be molecular changes in the very air itself. This would make it possible for guiding souls to such human beings, from their existence in the transition world shared with humans, to use the air to create a physical form for themselves, a form that was prepared by the *beliefs* of the human beings.

Only by "permission" of human ones walking in earth, and by the kind of accomplishment that we have described here, would guiding souls express, temporarily, through a physical form. As you would understand, it is a very rare occurrence.

QUESTION: Would you give us a specific method for communicating with our own guides?

To begin the process, your belief and assumption should be:

"Always, I am merged with my guiding ones."

For most, this merging remains unconscious. For those who desire to bring the merging between themselves and their guiding ones into their *conscious* awareness, to consciously communicate with guiding ones, the first step is, *love of yourself.*

If you do not love your own personality, you will most

likely tend to objectify, or separate your guiding ones as a force existing *outside* of yourself. The more brilliance and magnificence you ascribe to your guiding ones, the smaller you will feel within you own personality. You will begin to create a gap between your guiding ones and yourself, feeling, "I am the small one. My guiding ones are the brilliant, perfect ones."

So, the first step is love of yourself, day after day, forgiving the areas about yourself that you tend to judge and criticize, healing those areas. By loving your personality day after day, you are opening the door to your own soul, inviting it to come forth in *conscious* merging with you, just as it has always been in unconscious merging with you. You also invite into your conscious awareness the guiding souls that you have chosen to walk with you in this lifetime.

Next, to create a conscious communication with your guiding ones, you would need to establish a specific period of attunement in silence, once each day. You would choose the time of day and the length of time to spend.

You would begin your attunement period with a relaxation of your physical body.

Then, to the best of your ability, you would gently and patiently release your thoughts.

Next would come the all important step of creating feelings of love. You would begin by loving yourself. To help you do this, speak to your mind and say:

"I rejoice in the goodness in me. I rejoice in my desire for good. I rejoice in my creativity. I rejoice in my ability to love."

Do whatever is necessary in order to create feelings of love for yourself, within yourself.

Then, gently say to yourself, "I now desire to release earth for a few moments." If you choose, you can imagine that you are floating upward from earth. You may desire to imagine that you are floating in a sea of love. What is important here is to do something that turns your conscious awareness away from your earth life.

Next, you would create a feeling of being a reservoir of love. Imagine that you are filled with love, and you are asking for more. Notice the *addition* of love in that moment. This may feel like a gentle pressure, or warmth within your chest. It is a stream of love being added to the pool of love that is your own being. This stream of love, or this small wave of energy, is always flowing into the love of your being. But now, you are attempting to bring it to your conscious awareness, so that you can *feel* it.

Perhaps you will feel this wave of love very minutely at first. Over a period of time, it can grow to a large swelling of love within your feelings. This is the inflowing of love from your guiding ones.

We suggest that you begin your attunement to your guiding ones by focusing upon your *feelings*, for thoughts can be quite confusing. After a number of months, if you are satisfied that you can, at will, enter into a close attunement to this force of love that is the guiding ones to yourself, then, quite patiently, you could begin to say:

"Let me feel some *meaning* from this infusion of love from my guiding ones. Let me receive a sense of a goodness that will help me in my life."

This sense of meaning can be very vague at first. Simply work with it patiently. It will take time to gain a clear understanding in your thoughts. Perhaps, in time, when you have ended your attunement, you may be left with a thought that seems important. You might think, "Perhaps I need to give more to others." Then you could say, "Perhaps this is guidance." But, remind yourself that guidance comes *from within you*. Do not separate yourself from your guiding ones by saying, "There is a voice that speaks to me. That voice is my guiding ones. But I cannot trust my own thoughts. There are feelings of magnificence that come from guiding ones, but my own feelings are quite small and insignificant." To do this would bring great confusion, and even fear and pain.

Continue to rejoice in the *love* that you receive in your attunement process. The love is much more important than receiving thoughts of brilliance, or words that you ascribe to guiding ones. For it is the love that you desire and need. The thoughts, you are quite capable of creating yourself.

In any moment of your life, no matter what fear or pain you might be creating, you can remind yourself:

"I am filled with the love of the force that is God itself. That is my being. That is my nature. Also, I am loved by guiding souls who walk with me in this very moment. I rejoice in this love. I celebrate this love."

As you learn to *feel* this reality more and more, you will begin to consciously align with the many magnificent eternal forces that guide you moment by moment through your lifetime. From this opening, you will experience the inspiration and love that you need to feel in your human pathway.

In this moment, let yourself feel that all guiding souls to all ones in earth do rejoice that you desire the fuller knowledge of life, and that you are beginning the opening that will eventually bring you freedom and total fulfillment. In this moment, feel these beloved guiding souls coming forth to pour their love into your heart. Feel that from this love you will grow into truth.

In this moment, accept the love, and rejoice in it. This love is the key to all truth. It is the key to the understanding of your own being, of souls, of all of life. Feel the love that is God itself, and rejoice in it.

Chapter Four

EDUCATION

Teaching Our Children, Teaching Ourselves

As we turn our attention with you now to the challenge of causing human beings to respond in the ways that you would consider to be *educated*, you would need to begin with a sense of what is *un*-educated. Many times, the challenge that you ones face in *teaching*, particularly in teaching the children of yourselves, is the belief that the un-educated student begins with *ignorance*. This confused belief causes you to feel that if you are not successful in your teaching, then you have left ignorance in place. Therefore, many of your motives for teaching are rooted in *fear*—fear that you will not accomplish enough good to eliminate ignorance. So, before you begin to consider who you shall teach, and what you shall teach them, you need to look at your own *motives* for teaching those that you consider to be uneducated.

Let us begin our look at education by establishing some clarity about certain human categories of designation. First, let us agree that there is a certain human experience that you call *learning*, in which one gains new knowledge and understanding of life.

In other areas, you will have what you would call *teaching*. In teaching, one will intentionally impart to another, knowledge, or information, or beliefs, or techniques for living life.

What most human beings would consider to be *education* is a *formalized* teaching that is built around certain goals that are generally identified, although many times the goals are unclear, or they are simply vague, accepted traditions. There is a certain teaching that is always taking place in human life. You either teach consciously, or you unintentionally teach by the example of your human expression in your day to day life. At times, you might consciously teach, for example, teaching a friend how to fish, but for our purposes, that would not be considered education. Let us call education those areas of teaching in which at least a small group of human beings agree upon some intentions and goals for the teaching, and, they generally define a student group.

Of course, the most obvious example of education in your society is that which is established and *institutionalized* by human choice. Generally, such institutions are established by the choice of communities. These areas are the most familiar to all human beings. From the beginning educational structures for the small child, to the advanced structures for the adult, these areas of formalized, institutionalized teaching are what you would consider to be education.

It is important for you, in your own mind, to make a distinction between education and teaching. Because of your institutions, when you approach *education*, you have a greater need for human *agreement* than when you *teach*. When you teach, you have a certain individual freedom in what you can do. But, if you say, "I wish to launch an educational system," your challenge will be to find agreement amongst the human beings that you wish to help you. If you do not find such agreement, first of all, you will not be able to create your system. Secondly, you will not be able to change the system when it needs change.

There are several categories of focus that often become confused in your management of your present educational systems. First of all, you have the educational *system* itself, which, as you can observe, often becomes more important than the students within it. Those who are concerned with systems will often have difficulty understanding *individuals*. Those who are fond of working with individuals will often have challenges with systems.

If you are one who wishes to understand the education of your present country in a larger way, and you are quite serious about your understanding, then you will need to understand both areas—educational systems, and, the individual students within those systems. If you focus only upon one of these, your vision will be distorted.

Now, let us look at the human beings who are to be

taught by the educational system. Let us call them the *students*, whether they are small children or adults.

Often, as you have seen, bringing students together with an educational system does not always accomplish the designated goals of education. Many times there are intervening factors that need to be mastered in order to successfully educate the students. This, then, leads us deeper into the *human* part of the educational equation.

No matter how much effort is expended on your educational systems, without an understanding of human beings, and the way that human beings learn and grow, you will never produce the result that most of you desire, which is, intelligently educated, sensitive human beings. What many of you have already discovered, and others are now beginning to discover, is that *education* is not the most important focus. Your focus needs to be upon human existence—human beings. You are beginning to realize that, without an understanding of human beings—their needs, their desires, the ways that they grow and learn—you could have the most perfect educational system, but it would be misaligned with the students that you wish to teach.

Let us now address a very important area of knowledge about human beings. This is often the most difficult area for many to understand. Yet, the absence of understanding here is the largest single factor that undermines the most wonderful intentions of those who wish to educate human beings. This particular area, in human words, would be described as the need to understand: *What is a human being?*

First of all, this has to do with *your attitudes toward yourself.* Whatever you consider yourself to be as a human being, that is what you will project upon others. For example, there are now many upon this earth who focus upon teaching—particularly the teaching of younger children—with the attitude that, to speak playfully, the children are "uncivilized savages." They are empty vessels. They are ignorant children. This is what the teaching ones believe that they themselves were as children. So, the intentions of the teaching ones are distorted by their misunderstanding of what a human being is.

To educate properly, you will need to be willing to believe that even a newborn infant is not an empty vessel. You will need to believe than an infant, in some cases, can bring forth more wisdom than you yourself have accumulated as an adult. Without the understanding that *a human being is a temporary manifestation of an eternal soul who has walked on earth many times in human form,* it will be extremely difficult for you ever to fully build an educational system that does what you desire for the whole child. This means that there is a great deal of work to do, in terms of teaching those who have convinced themselves that human life begins at birth, and ends at death, and that there is nothing more.

If you begin with the attitude that a human being, beginning as an infant and child, is an empty vessel, or something to be molded into the shape *that is most desired by those who have established the educational system,* not only do you confuse yourself, but you carry upon your shoulders a responsibility that can never be met. You can never fully educate an *animal*, an empty being that has no base of inner wisdom.

The understanding of what a human being truly is will be slow in coming. However, many are already seeing clearly that in education, you begin with a child that is comparable to a large chest filled with *treasure*. If you are not familiar with such a chest, you might think, "What a worthless chest," and you throw it away and find somewhere else to start. If you are familiar with such chests, you know that they are filled with treasure. You know that your only challenge as a teacher is to *open the lock*. You can trust that the extraordinary capacities that live in all children only need to be pointed to.

You *do* need to teach each new child in this present lifetime the *rules* of human life, for the rules have changed since that child last walked on earth. The eternal souls who overwatch earth have "agreed" that as you come forth as a human infant, you will put aside your memory of the past so that you can be fully, if you will, "indoctrinated" into the present cycle of human expression and culture. Otherwise, you would have ones who would still insist upon throwing Christians to the lions. You would have others who would insist upon a certain kind of autocratic rule based upon an inherent nobility passed by birth from Pharaoh to Pharaoh.

So, it is quite efficient that each child comes forth to agree to begin human life with what *appears* to be an emptiness that needs to be filled. Filling this apparent emptiness with teachings about the present rules of life is a process that you ones have become familiar with. And these are the areas in which education is very important. However, you need to keep in mind that you are simply educating for the *present* generation. Your task is not to instill *perfection* in a child. That perfection already exists. Your task is to draw forth your sense of what is important in your present society, and then teach it to your children. What you consider to be important will be based upon your own personal feelings about life, and what you value. If you have learned to value nothing, then you will find nothing to teach your children. For example, if you have not learned to love, then you will not believe that it important to teach your children love.

In deciding what to teach in your educational systems, it is wise to always begins with *yourself*, either as a parent, a teacher, or one who supports education, looking to see what are your highest values. Then, you will need to try to implement those values into your educational systems. If you have no high values, then you have much to do in your own personality.

If you begin to search for "universal principles" to apply to education, you generally do this out of a sense that a child begins life as an empty vessel. And you assume that you must teach the child *everything*. However, if you could assume that *unconsciously* each infant brings forth a reservoir of, not only *human* experience from many past lifetimes on earth, but also extraordinary, let us say, "sets of balances" that are divine eternal forces that live inside the child's personality, then you could understand that if you never teach a child to read, or write, or function efficiently in your modern society, the soul of the child will still bring the child forth into important life experiences that you might say are the *purpose* of the child's life.

It is not your responsibility to *give* a child purpose and meaning. It is your responsibility to teach the child how to function efficiently in the present social context. It is your responsibility to make some intelligent judgments about what are the most important values of the present society.

Now, as you can see in *your* society, and in many of the scientifically based societies of the present world, all of you have generally agreed that what is important is *mastery of physical matter*, scientifically, economically, socially. Here, you must say, "If these are our choices, then these are our choices. If the choices do not please us, then let us change them."

We would say to you that education is a *human* affair. The forces of God do not say, "Educate your child in this way." Your challenge is not to discover the secret destiny forced upon you by God, or by any other force. Your challenge is to decide amongst yourselves what your highest values are. What is important in human life? And, in love, you would teach that to the ones that you believe need to learn it.

As you look at education, you have as a general focal point, *human beings making choices*. If you do not like the choices about education that your predecessors in your society have made, then change them and make new choices that more clearly reflect what you believe human beings should be taught by your educational systems.

Although your individual values and beliefs are important, as you look at your educational systems, you will need some guidelines beyond your own personal prejudice. Here, then, you must address the *variability* of human existence. In other words, you could understand that it would be quite delightful if you could impose your values upon the rest of the world. That would bring you a certain pleasure. But, you would also impose your narrowness, your lack of experience, your prejudice—your blind spots, so to speak.

If, on the other hand, you would come forth to strongly advocate the important choices that you believe need to be made in education, and you would also listen to other human beings, learn about them, understand them, and love them, then, gradually you would integrate a broad base of human choices from many different directions into your own understanding of education. This is essentially what you ones have done, at least theoretically. At times, in your educational structure, this process is usurped by those who would, in a sense, "steal" authority. But, for the most part, in your country, through a certain process that you might call *democratic*, you have allowed a large base of human choices to be brought together in your decision making about what you will teach, and to whom.

Although you might wish to find criticism here in this democratic process of education, you would first of all need to see the *effectiveness* of what you ones have created. For most people, it is easier to find fault than to find good. The faults glare at you. The good is usually overlooked. So, you might wish to begin addressing your systems of education with appreciation for how far you have come. At least you have organized the systems. You run them, if not always efficiently, at least they continue to run. They are in place. They move the children through them, from beginning to end. This, in itself, represents a rather large accomplishment, given the extraordinary complexity of the task of agreeing upon what you wish to teach, and how you wish to teach it.

It is always beneficial to begin with a bit of gratitude. Most of you will constantly underestimate yourselves and your true capacities. You will therefore underestimate your "products," so to speak, including your educational systems.

When it is time to address the *improvement* of your systems, you will always begin with your own personal values. If you had no personal values, you would not desire improvement. You would not notice that improvement is needed. So, you must have respect for the personal values that prompt you to desire to make changes in your educational systems.

Often, your desire for improvement begins with a *criticism*. You notice what you do not like, and you wish to change it.

For a few of you, it begins with a kind of deep idealism. You are aware of what you would like, and you try to change the system toward what you desire to see, what you believe is of greater value.

So, the primary reasons you would wish to change your educational systems are because you do not like what you see, or, you have a vision of more, and you wish to see your vision implemented. You might even switch back and forth between these two poles. No matter how and why you are prompted toward change, without a sense of your own *personal* involvement based upon your values, you would tend to focus upon *abstract issues* and lose your way, which has happened to many of you.

Once it becomes clear to you what is good in education, the next step is to *multiply* yourself. To find others who also believe in that goodness. You will need to realize that change in your educational systems comes about when human beings *agree*, particularly those human beings that you ones have made responsible for directing your systems. This means that you are moving into the cultural, political, and social arenas.

Many of you are quite idealistic, artistic, and sensitive, but you are not sophisticated in the cultural, political, and social areas. Therefore, you will not make much change in your educational systems unless you hire *advocates* that you align with the ones who are sophisticated in those arenas.

At a certain point, it becomes, not a challenge of *education*, but of *human behavior and motivation*. You need to be very clear about this. There are many people in your present society, even some who are involved in the educational system, who have strong, honest, and loving idealism, along with *ignorance* about the social process. They do not usually accomplish a great deal beyond their own personal sphere of influence.

Those who truly desire change in the educational systems must make a larger commitment to succeed in the cultural, political, and social areas in order to bring about *cooperation between human beings.* Otherwise, you must have an advocate to represent you and your position in those areas.

What we have touched upon so far has not emphasized *what* you teach, except that you identify for yourself what you personally believe needs to be taught, and how. Beyond this, we can begin to look with you now at what is important to teach human beings, particularly young human beings.

Given the patterns that we see in the human beings in your present society, and generalizing them for you, we would say that the first thing that you need to teach is *cooperation.* If you teach the small children to cooperate, and you teach them nothing about reading and writing, you will create a society that will please you. If you teach them everything about reading and writing, and nothing about cooperation, you will have, essentially, *your present society.*

Many have understood, and many can see that what we are saying, in essence, is that *you must teach your children to love.* Not that they would have strong, ecstatic feelings for one another, but that they would have a love that would say, "This is a valuable human being. I wish to understand them, to cooperate with them."

The second area that you need to teach has to do with a certain "transmittal" to the conscious awareness of the child, knowledge of *who the child is in this lifetime.* Although the child has a deep *unconscious* understanding of who it is, that knowledge needs to be brought to *conscious* awareness.

You will teach the child who it is, one way or another. You will teach consciously, or unconsciously. As we have suggested, most of the teaching that is now done teaches the child that it is an empty vessel, that it must listen to adults and obey them in order to know the truth. Many adults will unconsciously teach children to fear, to bend, to limit, to squeeze. All that the adults do, they will teach their children, and this will affect the child's sense of itself.

Until you can feel your own magnificence, you cannot honestly stand before a child and say, "What you are is a magnificent expression of God in human form." Instead, you will unintentionally say, "What you are is one who is unsafe, one who is threatened and in danger, and you must do this and that to secure your life, and make certain that it is not a painful life."

The third area that we would suggest that you teach is the area that we have pointed to earlier—the agreed-upon important values of your society. This can take you in many directions. In your society this usually has to do with valuing *accumulation of information,* and *intelligence*, particularly intelligence that is defined in terms of the ability to manipulate human words in speaking, reading, and writing.

However, if this is all that you teach, then you will create adults who are brilliant, but unfeeling. You might prefer a race of "idiots" who are loving. Of course, these are not the only choices.

The values that you emphasize will determine what

comes next, in terms of what you teach. Usually, in most of your educational areas, because of your values, you ones teach what is important from the *physical* point of view. This creates a focus upon money, security, professions, and attainments in the physical world. These are not always conscious choices, but they filter down from your values. Thus, most of what you teach is intended to create *successful* adults. And you begin by teaching your children to master the *tools* of success, which are *words*, and *abilities in the physical world*.

As you look at your present situation here, you could say, "If this pleases us, we will continue. If not, let us change it." There is no damage done to the *beings* of children by what you presently teach.

This leads to the next area that you would try to teach children, which is: In human life there can be a great deal of pain, but, *there is no damage to the child's being*. This is an extremely difficult lesson for most of you to teach, for you do not yet believe it yourselves. In your earth life, you ones have been trained to believe that you are in danger. You are in danger of poverty, illness, loneliness, death, and many other areas. You are convinced that such negative experiences will damage you, although this might not always be your *conscious* belief. You simply need to observe how frantically human beings try to avoid painful experiences and you will realize that they are convinced that pain will damage them.

Of course, your *physical bodies* can be damaged, so you will need to be concerned for them and protect them, and you will need to teach your children to do the same.

Yet, even the *death* of your physical body cannot damage your *being*. You are an *eternal being*.

To translate the teaching of being safe from damage into the present human context, you not only need to teach your children to love, to play, and to rejoice in life, but also *how to work with pain*. In general, most who teach young children are frightened for the children. They are frightened that they will send the children off into a harsh world. So, they overcompensate, and they try to always make perfection around the children. This teaches the children nothing about pain and what to do with pain.

We are not suggesting that you intentionally create chaotic situations for your children. But, when there is some pain that arises amongst the young children, those who teach the children need to take a moment to make the pain itself a lesson. They need to show the children how to be in pain. They need to teach: that pain is not bad; that the children need not be frightened of pain; that pain is temporary; and, that *pain can be healed*. These areas would be quite important as you guide the youthful ones. Even though you must begin with the attitude that you will try to protect children from pain if you can, and you certainly will try to guide them toward joy, creativity, and love, if pain *does* arise as a natural expression of their growing and learning, then it is a part of the curriculum, and it needs to be dealt with.

The next area has to do with a certain gradation, or *sequence* of projected learnings. You ones are most adept in this area, but this area is perhaps the least important of all that we have touched upon. This involves moving a child from one grade to the other, so that the learning is piled upon them in a sequential fashion—small learnings grow to large learnings, and, eventually, as adults, they can master an area.

What you fail to notice here is that most adults do not *remember* much of what they were taught in school, except the *process* by which they were taught. In your society, that process is usually quite harsh, quite competitive, and quite unfeeling in certain ways. So, even though you usually give your lives to facts and sequential learning, much of the learning is simply lost, for it is so unimportant to the children.

We are not saying that you must not teach intelligent sequences of knowledge. We are only suggesting that it is perhaps the least important thing that you do. Yet, in a way, some make sequential learning their *God*. You will even judge the quality of goodness of your children upon how brilliantly they can show you that they have learned their sequences—how brilliantly they can master the subject matter.

Here, again, the emphasis upon sequences is a matter of *human* values, and you ones must decide such things. But, we would suggest that if you can place the *content* of teaching after *the way that you teach*, then it does not matter what the content is. If you teach in an effective, loving way, children will become thrilled about whatever you teach. They will become excited and enthused. *They will learn even more than you believed you had to teach.*

What to teach and how to teach it are difficult areas for human beings. You ones have been struggling with these areas for thirteen generations. And, you most likely will continue to struggle for seven more. The struggle will continue until you have established new rhythms that are based upon *individual awakenings in the hearts of those who teach the younger children.* So, you might expect change to begin in the lower grades and "filter" up to the upper grades.

In general, when teaching adults, you will always focus upon *material content*, as it relates to the physical world, for you have not yet established education to open the *heart* of individuals, but to open their *minds*. So, in the future, to touch the heart, you will most likely establish a certain parallel educational structure that at present is called, "therapy." In the past, the structure that touched the heart was called, "religion." In the future, it will be called, "personal education." It will involve the teaching of *what it is to be human. What it is to be an expression of eternal forces, temporarily living in a physical body.*

Gradually, you will understand the importance of this touching of the heart, not only for the well being of the individual, but literally for the *success* of the individual in the physical world. You will begin to value the sense of confidence, competence, and fullness that infuses an individual as they gain a sense of their larger existence. And you will notice how such a sense sparks creativity. How it unleashes the human genius. And how it brings even more determination in life, rooted in confidence, rather than in fear.

Gradually, you will notice that the key to material success is not the harsh, disciplined approach of the educa-

tional systems of the past. Success comes from an understanding of your larger nature. Investigation of your
larger nature will most likely become popular, not because of your great idealistic impulses, but because of the
success that is achieved with such knowledge. The present
generation, as will a number of future ones, so values the
physical world that unless a thing leads to physical success, it most likely will not become a widespread shared
value amongst large numbers of human beings, at least in
your kind of nation.

We would say to you, as an individual: First, you have
the responsibility to teach *yourself.* Then, you have the
choice of becoming involved in educating large numbers
of people. Most of you will do one or the other. Some
both. These are *choices.* There is not a responsibility upon
you to teach children, to educate them. There is no badness in ignorant children. There is no badness in illiter-
acy. These are *human choices* that you ones value. You
value literacy. You value communicating in written and
formalized spoken words. Rejoice in your values. But, as
you look about, and you begin to sense the eternal nature
of yourself, and you begin to imagine that you are standing at the moment of your death, and you would say, "I
have dedicated my life to making certain that human beings can read and write," there will be a certain sense of
accomplishment in that, but, as you realize that you are
about to become an eternal soul—an existence in which
words are not necessary—you might have a sinking feeling
of having caught the wrong ship, and crossed the wrong
ocean. You might begin to feel, "I must return quickly

into earth, for *I forgot to teach them to love.*"

These values we cannot choose for you. But, you can ask yourself, "If I have only one thing to teach, what will it be?" Most of you will have several choices about what to teach. But, this kind of questioning of choices for your own life will help you place the important values first.

QUESTION: What are the essential elements that are absolutely necessary for being parents, the child's first teachers?

As you would imagine, the first element is *the willingness to share your being with the child*. This will come in varying degrees. The greatest challenge here is that most human beings allow *spontaneous feelings* to be the master of this area. If they do not spontaneously feel a perfect love for the child, they simply bemoan the fact, and they hope that someday they shall. They do not realize that the lack of depth of feelings of caring is caused by their own fears.

Most human beings will quite spontaneously deeply love their children. Their challenge is that they do not appreciate how important that love is. In other words, many intelligent, sensitive, loving parents will deeply fret and worry that they are not doing enough, when they are actually bringing warmth, love, and understanding to their children, which is their major promise to the child—a promise made inwardly, unconsciously, before they chose to bring that child into the world.

Even though there are some parents who allow their fears to create harshness that temporarily blocks the *ex-*

pression of their love, for most parents, the first necessary ingredient in teaching their children, assuming that they have the spontaneous love, is to appreciate how important the sharing of their being—their warmth, their love, and their presence—is to the child. They also need to have more trust in their own intuitive abilities and capacities to relate to the child, and to teach the child in a meaningful way.

There are some parents who will inflict their harshness upon their children. These are the ones who must be identified and hopefully taught, before they unnecessarily launch their child into earth with a distorted framework.

If the parents *do* inflict harshness upon the child, then you must assume that the soul of the child had "advance warning," so to speak, of that possibility. And you must also assume that even the harshest treatment by a father or mother will not damage the *being* of the child, although it might cause extreme suffering and distortion in the child's personality. It is this personality distortion that, as you can observe, is passed from generation to generation, particularly to those who commit violent crime. But, although you are fond of filling your communication media with these kinds of cases, they are actually quite small in number, compared to the large number of human beings who teach their children love in a rather kind way.

As a parent, you need to teach the same areas that we have been pointing to, particularly the sense of yourself as an eternal being, which is difficult for some. You need to be aware of your own values, and have confidence in them, although you need to be aware that values are very volatile and changeable. You have only to think of the ones that you had as an adolescent and realize that most of them are now gone. So, you would say to your child, when you are teaching overtly, "I *now* believe in this, and this is why. These are my feelings and thoughts about why I believe in this."

In teaching your children, there are some areas that you will *insist* upon. For most parents, these are the ingredients for a sense of normalcy and balance in social interactions. For example, you will insist that children do not beat their parents. You will insist that the child have a certain amount of respect and obedience for yourself and other adults. These values are so important, in terms of social harmony, that generally, they are not questioned, unless there is a great sense of guilt in the parent. A sense of guilt can cause parents to mistrust their own values and directions, and this will lead them to feel that they do not have the right to take authority over the child.

The next important task for parents teaching a child is to establish clearly, in your own mind, a certain sense of *direction* in life for the child. This can be quite loose and flexible. But, it is important, at least once each week, to say to yourself, "What kind of adult would I like to see this child become?" This is related to values, but it has to do with *intentions*, and *clarity about purposes*. In what direction do you intend to send the child? Here, you must be very gentle and subtle, for you do not wish to force the child in areas in which the child should be free to choose. You will focus upon *qualities of expression* as a human being, such as honesty, strength, kindness, and so forth.

You would not try to make life choices for the child that the child should be free to make. In other words, you would not say to a three-year-old child, "I am training you to be a bank manager." But, you could set your direction to train the child to be honest, strong, kind, and so forth.

The next area for the parents is to establish a sense of appropriateness, or rightness about the child's *environment*. You would do this almost naturally, without thinking about it. In other words, if you do not rejoice in ugliness and poverty, then you will do your best to create an environment for the child that is not that. These areas do not need much attention, except to remind you that if you do not make the choices *consciously*, then they will be made by default. If you would say, "I am too busy to be concerned with what environment this child has; the child will have whatever environment I have; I have too many pressing areas to consider this; I am too helpless to change this," then you will not have much to say about creating the child's environment. Here, you must balance your own personal needs and responsibilities against the choices that you will make for the child.

Beyond this, you enter into individual choices in the way that parents teach children. There are not structures that you can teach *all* parents to help them teach their children. For example, some human beings have come into earth life with a need to be quite abusive parents. This is a bit harsh when put into words, but, no matter how high *your* values might be for teaching children, as you can observe, there are some human beings who will have values that are quite low. And there is nothing that you can do about it, except to notice your response to such people. Notice whether you become frightened of them, or hate them, or whether you can continue to try to be of service to them, even though, most likely, you will be frustrated by them.

In this area of the parents of earth, it is good to delineate your ideals and try to communicate them, and work diligently to try to teach them. But, eventually, you must face certain limits that exist in the *physical* world. When you come to these limits, then it becomes your challenge to decide what to do. Do you fall into despair? Do you curse the limit? Do you curse those who cause it? Or, do you take your idealism and try to weave it with understanding and patience so that you can learn "alternative" responses for when your idealism is frustrated.

Inside yourself, you have many choices about how to teach your children. However, when you wish to find broad solutions for *many* parents to teach their children, then you are rather restricted in what you are able to do, except by example. If you wish to do more, then you can dedicate yourself to teaching parents how to teach their children.

QUESTION: What is the missing principle, or underlying purpose that we are working to uncover that will cause the shift we are seeking in education?

As all of you who are concerned with education hold your vision and communicate it to others, you will discover that the missing ingredient is *understanding for one another*. Many times, those who are most zealous about change and reform are the least understanding of the human beings that they consider to be blocking their pathway.

As you work to improve the way that you ones educate, if you establish the sense that you are engaged in a *battle*, then you will be busily looking to see who is an *enemy*, and who is a *friend*. But if you decide that you are engaged in *a cooperative endeavor*, then every human being involved needs to be cooperated with. There are no enemies. There are no *bad* groups or directions.

The missing ingredient of understanding for one another in the area of education is also what is missing in all of your society, when there is challenge. Without understanding for one another, you create the feeling that those who oppose your direction are your enemies. That they are the problem. You feel that they must be changed, or eliminated, or forced to recapitulate.

Once you understand that the forces of God that you so hunger to feel in your own life actually live in those very human beings that you believe are responsible for the flaws in your educational systems, then the secret ingredient becomes *your patience, and your capacity to love them, in order to gain their cooperation*. Of course, you must have a certain understanding of what you wish them to cooperate about. And these are the areas of defining values. In other words, you cannot go into an educational system and say, "This is a bad system, let us change it," and then not know what you wish to change it to. You need to have a certain amount of foresight, imagination, creativity, knowledge, wisdom, and experience in the educational area before you can be one with a solution that you ask others to cooperate with. Yet, even if you have no solution, you can still invite others to cooperate with you in order to help you create one.

The missing ingredient is not knowledge of education, or children, or human beings. The missing ingredient in your educational systems is: *the inability to identify with others to such a deep extent that you all become lovingly and creatively involved in the resolution of what you consider to be the problem.*

QUESTION: How can we learn for ourselves, so that we can teach children and teenagers, that they have no limitations, and that there is only joy and love and goodness, without abandonment and fear?

Let us imagine that you have come upon one large elephant in the jungle. And you are terrified that you will be stepped upon. So, you run away. Then you meet your child on the pathway, and you look frightened. Your child would say to you, "What has frightened you so?" Since you do not wish to appear to be a coward to your child, you would say, "It was a large herd of elephants coming upon me." You consider this only a slight exaggeration, but it causes you to appear much more courageous than you were actually able to be.

Most human beings are quite fond of being seen as magnificent and ideal. But, inwardly, at times, they do not feel their perfection. Most of you are quite adept, at times, at seeing what you hope you will be, but you have not yet mastered being that. You have begun. You have tested certain areas. But, still, you are frightened. You are not secure in certain areas. You do not feel your *own* magnificence. Therefore, you cannot teach children their magnificence.

When you come to your inner life—particularly thoughts and feelings about larger truths, values, being, and existing—these areas are much different than your physical earth affairs, which you can teach intellectually. In the inner area, you can effectively teach only what you have *lived*, not what you simply believe, or know intellectually. You can say to others, "I *believe* that we are the perfection of God in human form." But, to truly teach this to a child, you must *know* it, and *feel* it, and *live* it. This does not mean that you must live it perfectly every moment. But, at least for enough moments so that when you are with children, you can interact with them from that feeling of your own magnificence.

This is not so much an area of *teaching*. This is an area of *demonstrating*. If you are with your teenage child and you are feeling, "I have not done enough; they do not love me deeply enough," then you are teaching them that you feel inadequate and guilty. And you will most likely trigger their capacity to feel inadequate and guilty.

In those feelings, however, there is much learning. When you have learned the principle of honesty, you would say to them, "Today, I am *feeling* so inadequate and guilty. I so wish that we could have perfect love, but it seems to me that there is a gap between us." Then, you are teaching them honesty. And they will know that the beloved father or mother to them also knows fear, guilt, and inadequacy, and has the courage to approach it. If you are honest about your negative feelings, your children will learn that there is nothing to be frightened of in such feelings.

By learning to heal negativity, children can eventually learn that they are eternal beings who cannot be damaged by the negative experiences of life. They will learn that they are safe, that they are secure, that there is nothing in life that can damage their being. When you have feelings such as these and you are living them, then share them with your children, and that will be an effective teaching.

The teaching of larger truths is a rather vague and cloudy area. It depends upon individual human personalities—how you ones choose to live your lives. There is no way to say to a child, "You are an eternal being, life cannot destroy you," other than to say it. But, that does not mean that they understand it, or feel it. Saying it is only a beginning point. Living it honestly is the real teaching.

So, if you are frightened by one elephant, and you say to your child, "I was frightened by one elephant," then, when they see one elephant and they are terrified, they will feel, "My feelings of fear are not so bad, for my father and mother were terrified by one elephant." In other words, *they will not feel a pressure to be more than you have been able to be in your movement toward idealism.*

QUESTION: Some people feel that *public* education in the United States has been generally disappointing in its ability to produce an educated, capable generation

to manage our society. There have, however, been isolated instances of successful educational systems in the *private* sector. What can we do individually and collectively to create structures that will make these successful private programs more widely available?

Looking at the challenges that you see in the public schools, we will now generalize for a large number of different places and areas, but, some of the challenges that you see do not exist in all public schools. In general, the largest challenge in public education is the inability of teaching ones to establish *a sense of belonging with the students*. Of course, this does not apply to all teachers.

In the *private* educational area, there is a certain amount of authority invested in the *student*, by way of their family, because of the monies paid. So, there is a certain reduction of the feeling of gap between the teacher and student. Again, this is a generalization that is not always true.

If you wish to spread the success that has been attained in more exclusive schools of a private nature, you would need to find a way to bridge the gap between teacher and students, so that the teacher is not an authoritarian dictator standing before those who are considered inferior because they are not yet educated. This has to do with many complexities of teaching teachers.

There is also the challenge of the *disciplinary* aspect of the present public schools. Here, you would need to teach teachers to work with their fear of the harshness, volatility, and rebelliousness of certain students. In many cases, where there are the students from the less sophisticated

cultures and environments, the students have learned responses that are frightening to teachers. The students have
behaviors that are threatening to the personal well being
of teachers. This is another reason why there is a gap between the teacher and the student.

Until the teacher becomes a *friend* to the student, most
likely you will not have what you desire in the public
educational areas. This is not a criticism of the teachers.
Many times, the hostility within students would make it
almost impossible for there to be the closing of the gap so
that the teacher could become a friend. In such cases, you
simply must wait until you have learned to teach younger
children more effectively how to cooperate, or, you must
tolerate the gap between teacher and student, and the
ensuing challenges that arise from it.

You could make all manner of adjustments in various
teaching methods used in the public schools, and, if the
teachers continue to come forth with the gap between
themselves and the students, even though an improved
method might cause a bit of improvement in the classroom
results, it will not result in what you desire. Rather than
methods, the focus needs to be upon the *human relationship between teacher and student.*

In general, in the private school areas, because of the
"obligation" owed by the teachers and administrators to
the fee payer, which is usually the parents of the child,
there is usually more restraint and patience on the part of
the teacher. The relationship between the teacher and the
student is improved. And, in general, there is a more satisfactory training of the student.

QUESTION: Television has become an inevitable part of our lives. How can we counteract the negative effects of television upon our children?

First of all, in the individual home, you have the obvious choice of limiting the child's exposure to the television. Let us compare this to the difference between jumping into the water from a ship to have a leisurely swim, and jumping from a sinking ship to save your life. In other words, a more creative way can be found to address the problem, but, failing that, you would take the emergency step of simply limiting the exposure to television of yourself as an adult, and of your children. You would monitor the fare for your children, and you would make conscious decisions about what they watch, not allowing your own sense of busyness and preoccupation to cause you to leave the child to its own devices.

Secondly, you would work diligently to establish a kind of *running response* with your children to what you see on the television. If you monitor the viewing of certain programs, and you arrange that questionable programs are viewed together, then you *respond* to what you see in a natural way, communicating to the child, for example, "I am so upset that this one on the television did cause pain to that one. I do not find that amusing, or interesting, or entertaining."

Now, this responding is a delicate area. You cannot moralize, or pontificate. But, you can deeply share your own *feelings*. Gradually, you will begin to establish a certain kind of training of the child, showing the child that the power to *respond* to the content of television is extremely strong. No matter what you ones feed one another on your televisions, *there will be always the inner power of the human being to respond in ways that are aligned with your ideals.*

So, not only do you have the power to refrain from engaging in questionable viewing, but, if you do engage, you have the power to *change* the impact by your response. You have the power to use your response as a training, as a teaching for the child.

However, in the long run, you will not find a great deal of improvement in the content of your television until you find a way to communicate to those who make the choices and decisions, to convince them that there is a *larger need* in human beings that is not being met by television. This larger need is for a deeper understanding of life, and it is shared by many human beings. However, here again, just as with the educational systems—and this will generally be true of any human endeavor in which control has been taken into the hands of a small number of individuals—you will need to realize that in trying to make change in the content of television, you are not dealing with education, or even art. You are in an area of political, social, and economic concerns. And you will only make change by gaining mastery in those areas.

If you do not wish to work diligently to master those areas, then you will not be one who makes change in television. Most human beings will not be willing to work hard enough to make a change, so they will simply have the power of *response* for themselves, and for their children.

QUESTION: Education is more than fundamental learning, books, lessons, and so forth. There seems to be a spiritual element that actualizes the information being taught into useful truths of life. Please give us, as adults, an attunement that would help us best tap into this spiritual realm, so that we can feel more confident about how and what we teach, and to help us become more useful vehicles of truth in our everyday lives.

Here is an extremely delicate area, for if we would say the truth to you quite baldly, we would need to say that the spiritual element is activated most clearly when you do not find fault with what you presently find fault with. However, we do not wish to tip you toward *passiveness*. In other words, there is a great value in identifying what does not please you in all areas, particularly your educational areas. And it is valuable to strive to change what does not please you. But, the truth is, it does not matter to your *soul* whether you change it or not. It matters to *you as a human being*. What matters to your soul is, *how you live* while you strive to change it.

If you come forth into the area of education and you feel that you can make a perfect educational system by imprisoning those who have caused the damage in the present one, you might create a wonderful educational system, but what you will learn is *hatred*, *resentment*, and *lack of love*. If you come forth and decide, "Education is not important, but love is," and even if you have a generation of "idiots," you have tapped a certain kind of *freedom from fear* that might be more important than education.

These are not values that you ones will likely act upon. Here, we are simply attempting to show you that when you ask, "What is the spiritual area of education, and what is the important spiritual element," you are entering into an area that is *already* filled with forces of God. No matter what you ones do as human beings in your education of one another, all human beings are already filled with the forces of God. Nothing can change that.

If you teach your children to murder one another, their beings are still filled with the forces of God. The murder does no damage to their *beings*, for they have died in many past human lifetimes on earth, and they have survived those deaths.

However, the challenge here is that this is not a profitable way for a human being to think. In other words, if you would say, "It does not matter because all is God," you essentially negate the entire purpose of human life, which is *to make choices*. So, it is very important to notice what you do not like, and to dedicate yourself to changing it. Work in diligence toward that change. But, remind yourself that you do not need to fear *failing*, for if you do fail to change what you believe is wrong or bad, that area is still filled with the forces of life, the forces of God.

As we have said, this is a very delicate area. When it is time to approach your educational area—the education of yourself, and the education of your children and your adults—you must be willing to make your human choices. Know that your human choices will not change the magnificent *eternal realities* that live in all human beings. But, your choices will change *human life*. And they will change that life in the direction that you wish it to go, if you are vigorous enough.

So, when you ask, "What is the spiritual way to open and teach?" know that the spiritual way is: *To believe that nothing can damage you, or your children.* Not even a bad educational system. Not even a complete absence of education. Nothing can damage the *being* of you and your children.

The key then to *teaching* the spiritual truth is to teach: *The forces of God are perfect and unchangeable.* The forces of love that stream into you can never be diminished. The human *emotions* can rise and fall, but the eternal forces that live within you can never be diminished, or limited.

If you say, "I take up the cause of defining the spiritual truth, and living it, for me and for those in earth," then there will be certain values that you as a human must give allegiance to, such as love, honesty, and sensitivity to others. You will try to make changes according to those values. And, at the same time, you must have the courage to believe that the areas that you are unable to change are not bad or wrong.

As you work individually each day, first it is of greatest benefit to do your *human* duty, and make your choices. As you arise each morning, clarify your choices by asking yourself:

"What do I value in this day? What do I stand for? What do I live for?"

Your values might include teaching children, or making money, or gaining political office. Your highest value might be to sing, or dance, or write, or worship God in a religious context. Whatever you do, the most important thing is to be *clear* about what you value in life.

Next, it is important that your human choices *please* you. If they do not, then *change them*. Make choices that please you, then follow those choices.

The next important focal point is: *To try to feel your own eternal nature.* It is of little value to have large spiritual ideas and ideals when you cannot *feel* the love that is God stirring inside your own heart. If you cannot feel the forces of God inside of you, then you will not see God in others. You will not find God in life. Before you try to teach in ways that draw upon the spiritual truths of life, it is so important to learn to feel God as a force of love in your own heart.

After this comes *action*. You would try to *act* upon the values, choices, and spiritual experiences that you have. If in each day you define your human choices and commitments, and you gain clarity about them, and you also take time to feel the forces of God in you, then we can promise you that your actions in earth will be extremely beneficial and effective, whether they are turned toward education, toward business, toward art, toward philosophy, toward any human endeavor. Your actions in earth life will be magnificent.

As you contemplate your own existence as a single human being—a human being who perhaps at times struggles to understand the complexity of life, particularly as it involves the social interactions and the education of other human beings—say to yourself:

"Whatever I think, and feel, and do in the future in all of these areas of my life depends upon *how I feel about myself in this moment*. If I feel that I am small, incompetent, impotent, or unworthy, then everything is diminished. If, in this moment, I am willing to put aside my own self-criticism and negativity, and I am willing to feel that *I am the beauty of God in human form*, then everything that I do throughout this lifetime will be augmented."

In the final analysis, in the educational area, and in your human living in *all* areas, what is most important is *what you feel* in each moment of your life. If you feel small and limited, then work with those feelings, share them with others, and *heal* them. If you feel the beauty and magnificence of life, then work inwardly to *expand* those feelings. This simple way of working with your feelings, both positive and negative, can guide you day by day, throughout this lifetime.

For this moment, make a gentle relaxation within yourself. Encourage a deep feeling of love inside yourself. Imagine that everything that has troubled you throughout this entire lifetime has suddenly vanished. Your past troubles simply do not exist. In this moment, if you do not re-create that negativity in your thoughts, feelings, and imagination, then the negativity does not exist in this moment.

Now, let yourself feel that the greatest learning that you can make for yourself as a human being, and the greatest teaching that you can share with others is this:

You are an eternal soul, temporarily living in human form. The past continually falls away behind you, and the perfection of God constantly fills you, and animates you in the *present*.

If you would learn this, and live it, and teach it to others day by day, then all of the human choices that you make in this lifetime would blossom into the magnificence that was intended for this earth.

Chapter Five

HEALING ADDICTIONS

A Spiritual and Psychological Approach

To help you work with your present personality, in terms of how you draw human fulfillment to yourself in this lifetime, we will begin by looking closely with you at your *desires*. In order to bring greater clarity and understanding to this area, we will explore the way your human desires unfold in this lifetime. We will suggest a "range of desiring" that you can use as a guide for unfolding your desires, and for monitoring and working with the desires that seem to overpower you at times—the areas that can become a fixation, or an obsession, or, what you might call, an *addiction* in the human life.

In working with your desires, first of all, it is necessary to *respect* your desires. This is particularly important for those who have an addictive desire. For such ones, there is usually a tendency to become suspicious of your desiring, to feel, "My strong desires are what are leading me astray and causing me challenge in this period of time."

To respect your desires, you must understand that it is the forces of God itself that flow into you and animate your awareness and your being inside your body, allowing you to think, to have emotions, and also to make a strong stirring in you to *desire* in this lifetime. So, in a simple way of speaking, your desire *energies* are actually forces of God.

However, the *content* of your desire is decided by human *choice*. In other words, the fact that you can strongly desire a thing comes from a feeling that rides upon the energy of God. *What* you desire depends upon what you have decided is important to you in the physical world, which will affect your human choices. At times, human choice can distort desires. For example, if the forces of God would prompt you to desire love in this lifetime, and you become confused and desire only sexual fulfillment, then you have made a distortion in the desire energy.

Let us look now at the *range* of human desiring. First, you have desires that are linked with your *animal* nature. Such desires are beneficial for moving your physical body—which is your animal portion—through the physical world in a most effective and appropriate manner. These are your strong desires to feed your body, to drink, to rest, to procreate through sexual union, and so forth. These desires have a relatively strong force in most human beings. Such strong desires would be in the "normal" range of desiring.

If you have a strong appetite in each day, and you satisfy it by an intelligent choice of the food that you eat, then you are in the normal range of desiring. But, if each day you feel, "I am so sad," and you have a raging appetite for food to quench the sadness in you, and it becomes uncontrollable, then you might say that you have an addictive desire for food. In such a case, what is ordinarily a normal, beneficial, animal desire to sustain your body becomes intensified to the point where it becomes a challenge to you.

You need to become familiar with your own inner feelings of desire so that you can answer the questions: "What is normal and acceptable to me in terms of the strength of my animal desires? What is an *exaggeration* of my normal desires?" Learning to be sensitive to yourself is an important part of learning how to master your desires.

Next, you have desires that are quite individual to you personally, that grow out of the unique circumstances of your particular life, and that will affect your animal desires. In other words, if you would say, "I desire the pizza pie," that is your particular manifestation and alteration of the basic animal desire for food.

Let us say that you are obese in your body shape, and that you have translated the basic desire for food into a passion for fats. Then, you would see that you are out of balance, in terms of the normal, healthy desiring in the food area. If you feel, over a long period of time, "I cannot live without fats,'' and you eat them constantly, then you might have an addictive desire in the food area.

The same is true of your personal preferences in other physical desire areas. You will place your particular stamp upon your animal desires. For example, if you respond to the ordinary sexual desire by translating that into a desire to copulate with animals, then you might say that you have placed a distorted and unusual stamp upon the normal desire for sexual fulfillment.

In these areas, you will need to learn to clearly sense your ordinary desire levels, and you will need to discover how your inner personality patterns affect your normal desiring. Whether your patterns are positive or negative to you, you will need to learn how those patterns extend your desiring into healthy or unhealthy areas.

There are some desires that are natural to human beings, and they are not associated with your animal nature. They are associated with your eternal nature. Such desires are stimulated by impulses from your own soul, from guiding souls to you, and from the forces of God itself. Some of these impulses are general in nature, and usually apply to all human beings. Some are quite specific to your own soul. First, we will look at the impulses that are general in nature.

In general, we could say that all human beings are implanted with a desire to love and to be loved, and to seek companionship and harmony with other human beings. This interweaves with your own personal desires for self indulgence. Here, your normal range of response to the impulse of eternal forces, if you were not confused in your personality, would be to have a moderate desire to love other human beings, and to be loved by them. However, your own personal influence can diminish this impulse in your personality, causing you to have a very weak desire to love others. In that case, you do have a challenge of desiring.

You can also intensify this impulse by the way that you work with your personality patterns. This would result in a very strong personal desire to love others, and to be loved by them. This could either benefit you, or it could be a challenge, depending upon how much fear there is in your motives. If you are passionate about kindness, love, and harmony because you genuinely desire to give to others, and to create beauty in the world, then that would be a strong positive personal adjustment to the average human desire that you would make inside your personality. On the other hand, let us say that you are feeling weak, impotent, and unworthy, and you have developed an obsessive need to be loved by others. This might cause you, out of fear, to exaggerate the natural impulse to love. Then you have a challenge in desiring. This could even become an addiction to being loved and approved of by others.

So, your personal adjustment of the natural impulse to love others and to be loved by them can either benefit you, or challenge you. You will need to learn how your particular personality patterns affect this impulse within you so that you can recognize and heal any blockages here.

There is another impulse from your soul, from guiding

souls, and from God, that, in human words, would need to be called, an impulse to know the truth about life. All of you, within your personality energies—your personality matrix—have been implanted with an impulse to cause you to desire to know the truth of your eternal nature, and to explore such issues and questions as: Why are you walking on the earth? Where will you go after your death?

Here, again, the moderate desire to know truth would be the average, normal response to this impulse, for this impulse is not intended to override your important human purposes in the physical world. It is intended to merge with those purposes.

In this area also, your personality patterns can alter the moderate, normal desire. You can become very passionate about knowing truth and discovering spiritual realities, and this can benefit your human life, if you integrate it with your daily physical affairs and relationships. If you become confused and begin to be obsessed with the spiritual world, then you can unknowingly, and unintentionally withdraw from the intensity of human physical life without realizing that living that intensity is one of your purposes on earth.

There are many other general impulses from eternal forces that affect your relationship with life, but the ones we have mentioned are the strongest. Most of the others have to do with such areas as, seeking out community, coming forth with desires for altruism and kindness— those kinds of patterns. All of the eternal impulses that live within you need to be monitored by you, and you need to understand how your personality patterns interact with those impulses so that you can adjust your patterns when you feel that they are out of balance.

In the *personal* area of the eternal impulses, or soul energies that we have called "desires," that are implanted in your personality—particularly by your own soul as a part of your plan for your present human lifetime—these could be quite varied. Here, we can simply point out the area, to remind you that you do have such soul energies and impulses within you. You will need to work patiently each day with your own inner patterns of thought and feeling in order to decide what are the particular desires that have been stimulated in you by your soul.

To help you understand certain ways to approach this, imagine that in a certain male one, his soul might place into his personality matrix, before his birth, a strong desire to teach others about God. But, such a desire impulse would always be quite broad in nature. In other words, the desire impulse from his soul to himself would not say: "You must become a Catholic Priest," or, "You must become a Jewish Rabbi." The impulse would be intended to communicate to him in a way that would simply say, in effect, "You have a great passion to teach about God."

Then, the human personality of this male one must, first of all, let that desire, which has been prodded by the soul energies, come to the surface—to his conscious awareness—so that he can feel it, and recognize it. Then, his personality must make some choices about how to fulfill that desire. He must say for himself, using his will, "This is how I *choose* to teach about God." He might choose to stand on the street corner and preach. Or, he might choose to write books. He might choose to engage in philosophical pursuits of knowledge about God.

Your human personality is filled with strong impulses from your own soul that your soul "hopes" will prod you to bring certain desires to the surface, and then to decide what you wish to do about those desires. Those impulses have to do with purposes that you have brought from past lifetimes, and that your soul hopes you will accomplish in this lifetime. The impulses also, in smaller numbers, have to do with challenges. For example, a female one might be implanted with a tendency to desire alcohol. The purpose of that tendency is for her to bring those desire patterns to the surface so that she can heal fears that are associated with them. But, in her confusion, she might respond in ways that do not heal the fear, and she may become addicted to the alcohol. There can be such impulses from the souls that will, at times, involve tendencies toward strong desires that are not intended to be carried forth and fulfilled. Instead, the impulse is intended to prod the personality to heal the unbalanced desire and the fears associated with that desire.

This gives you a broad understanding of how desires are living inside you. This will help you study yourself and your desires. Always work lovingly with your desires, never criticizing yourself, or harshly condemning yourself. If you would take a harsh, negative approach to your work, then, it would be better not to study desires at all. If you intend to study your desires and truly master them—particularly to heal addictive desires—then you must make a promise to yourself to be gentle and loving with yourself while you study your personality patterns, and while you heal the confusing ones.

QUESTION: What is it that causes strong desires to move to the point of addiction, where they seem to take on a life of their own and control the person, rather than being controlled by the individual?

There are several general areas here that we can point to that apply to all human beings. Then, some individuals will have their own unique reasons for driving themselves to addiction. But, the generalizable causes of addiction can be very beneficial for you to understand.

In general, the primary reason that desires become addictive is: *there is not enough joy and fulfillment in your day to day, ordinary life.* Usually this is connected to: a lack of love in your heart for yourself; and, not enough love from others. It is often connected to a feeling of lack of purpose and meaning in your life.

Often, wealthy ones who have all that earth could physically offer, if they do not open their creative inner selves to the areas that we have mentioned, they will seem to waste away. They can become addicted to physical pleasures, for there is no other sense of purpose in their lives.

So, that which causes one to feel, "I must eat so much, I must numb myself with alcohol, I must have the drugs in my system, I must constantly engage in sexual activities," is essentially a sense that there is no other fulfillment in life. There is no deep purpose and meaning. There is no deep love or joy. They feel, "My life is so flat and empty." And, as these kinds of responses grow, at times, they become so strong that they go a bit further, and the feeling is, "Not only is my life empty, but now it is very painful."

Thus, another strong influence upon addictions, particularly the addictions to alcohol and drugs, is: the deep feeling of pain and suffering that some carry in their hearts, and are unable to heal. This usually comes from the painful experiences of the present lifetime. For example, if there is one who is constantly beaten, abused, and humiliated as a child, and they grow up carrying suffering and pain in their heart, they will feel, "I must have some joy in my life." But, they cannot find joy in the ordinary areas of life, for their pain is so great. So, they will often find joyful pleasures that are very intense, such as the alcohol or the drugs, and that will tend to temporarily numb their feelings of pain.

As you work within your own personality each day, ask yourself: Are you so unappreciative of your life that you make a numbing of your feelings by taking yourself for granted? Are you so un-alert that you have let your pains fester and grow without healing them day by day? Have you let your pain become a dominant negative pressure upon you, so that you feel that the only way to have joy in your life is to have some intense physical pleasure stimulate your personality?

Another factor in addictions—particularly in this modern period, and particularly in the more affluent countries such as the United States—is a kind of habit that is connected to how easy it has become to fulfill your physical desires. When you have enough money, usually, you can have most physical things that you desire. And, usually, when your desires are strong, you fulfill them quickly. Over a period of time, this results in a need for instant gratification. You lose patience with working gradually toward desire fulfillment. You must have fulfillment instantly.

When this desire for instant gratification becomes very strong, it can confuse your work with your desires. For example, let us say that you desire a deep love relationship. It takes time to create such a relationship, to nurture it, and to come to deep fulfillment in it. But, you desire that kind of fulfillment immediately. Then, you may rush out and have only a sexual union, because you are not patient enough to nurture a full relationship to reach the deeper love.

Under the influence of this need for immediate gratification, some may say, ''I desire love, but it is so difficult and takes so much time. I believe I shall have the instant pleasure of food instead.'' Now, you usually do not say these things consciously. We are putting words to unconscious patterns. But, for some, after engaging in such instant gratification for a period of time, it seems much easier to eat, or smoke the cigarettes, or drink the alcohol for fulfillment than to create a deeply loving relationship, or to become a fine artist, or to have the joy of fulfillment in other areas that take more time and energy to achieve. Such ones simply fall into the habit of stimulating themselves with food, caffeine, nicotine, or other areas that can instantly be enjoyed, and the basis for addiction is established.

Even though the enjoyment of the instant pleasure is strong in its own way, all of the desire energy for the deeper, long-term fulfillments is transferred into the addictive area, which intensifies even more the desire for that instant pleasure. Thus, you can make a large thing out of a small pleasure, and you can say, "I *must* have my caffeine in the morning. I *must* have my cigarette every so often each day. I *must* have this or that." And, the more you ignore fulfillment in the deeper, long-term areas, the more important your addictions will become to you.

These are some of the generalizable patterns that most ones will manifest when they are creating addictive desires.

QUESTION: Some people are said to have an "addictive personality." They will heal one addiction, then develop another. They move from addiction to addiction. Are such people born with that type of addictive personality, or is it simply a manifestation of behavior?

First of all, let us look at some human beings who are born with a "neutral" personality. In other words, they do not bring into this lifetime any particular tendency toward excessive desiring that could become addictive. For such ones, most addictions that they develop will come from the factors that we have pointed to as the general causes of addictions. Their over-indulgences will come from: feelings of flatness in life; lack of purpose and meaning; too much passion for immediate pleasure; not enough love; or other general causes. So, even though some human beings will come into earth without a strong inherent tendency toward addiction, they can still "grow" addictions, so to speak.

There are some human personalities that come forth from birth, because of energies planted in them by their eternal souls, with an extraordinary *intensity* of desire. When they desire a thing, they desire it totally and completely, from small things to large things.

This intensity of desiring is not intended by the soul to be an impulse toward addiction. It is simply that the soul, for many reasons that are important to the soul, has created a passionate personality that wishes to plunge into life with total intensity.

If such individuals begin to become frightened and confused about life, and they stir up some of those patterns that lead to addiction, then they are more likely to develop addictive desires than one who is not so intense about life. So, what you would call an "addictive personality," is, in truth, an *intense* personality, who simply has extremely strong desires, and has not matured in the way of fulfilling those desires—they have not learned to balance their desires and fulfill them in areas that are healthy and beneficial.

These intense individuals are usually the ones that you will see, even from childhood, having a passion for everything that they desire. They might desire many of the sweets, they might play for hours and hours, totally and intensely. If they are friendly and loving, they will be extremely passionate and loving with their friends, and later with their deeper loved ones. If they are later focused upon desires to fulfill themselves in their career, they will throw themselves into it passionately. They might become the "workaholic." They might become the one who rises to the top of their career. These are the ones, when you see them experimenting with alcohol, who will be constantly inebriated, who never know when to stop taking the alcohol. Such individuals need to be taught *patience* and *balance*. They need to learn that their intense desire fulfillments can be achieved, but if they are not monitored, they will become addictive desires.

Fortunately, in terms of addictions, these intense personality patterns have a positive side. When such individuals decide to heal their addictions, they will usually do it intensely and passionately, and they will usually succeed dramatically in totally giving up their addiction. However, they often become the ones who are adamantly against such addictions. This would be the zealous reformed alcoholic, or reformed smoker.

The causes of addiction in intense personalities that we have looked at here are quite generalized, but you can recognize some of these patterns, perhaps in yourself, as well as in others.

Then, finally, there are some patterns that are placed into the personality by the soul as tendencies, that are related to past desire patterns that became addictive in other lifetimes before the present. For example, you might have one who was a priest in another lifetime, and who was so frightened of sexual expression because of his religious teaching that he developed an addiction to extremely rigid behaviors that are anti-sexual. Let us say that he developed an addiction to celibacy, in a very exaggerated and distorted way. Then, this one, in the present lifetime, might bring forth that same tendency and have a great challenge in the love area. Or, there might be one who was addicted to alcohol in the past, and perhaps met their death through overindulgence in the alcohol. They might be more prone in this lifetime to be addicted to strong drink or other substances.

There are important factors in your desire patterns that could exist in your personality from birth. Your duty, and your need, is to learn about them, discover any exaggerations that you might have because of them, and then, either alone or with others, learn to identify the fears that live beneath those patterns, and eventually heal the fears.

QUESTION: There is some evidence that addictions, particularly to alcohol, are hereditary. Some people believe that if your father, or your mother, or grandparents were alcoholic, then you have a greater chance of becoming an alcoholic. Would you speak about this?

This is as though you would look at a mule, and you have never seen a mule before, and you look only at the tail end, and you say, "A mule is for defecating," for you see only the eliminations of the mule. If you look only at the head, you might say, "A mule is for eating." If you see the whole mule, you might say that it is for eating and eliminating. In other words, what you see will depend upon your perspective.

Because you cannot see that the genes in each human body are actually controlled by eternal souls, that they are manipulated for the souls' purposes, then you might say, "This male one is an alcoholic because it is passed through the genes from his father to himself." However, if you look at it from a different perspective, you could say, "The soul of this son desires him to heal the tendency toward alcoholism, therefore, this soul will choose as a father, a human being who is an alcoholic, and this will be the mechanism whereby the tendency to alcoholism is triggered in the son."

If you would say, rigidly, "Genes transmit alcoholism," this means that every alcoholic would have alcoholic children, which is not the case. So, be flexible here, and know that what you would call "genetic" forces are, in truth, soul forces. And, the souls, at times, will use genetic structures to accomplish their purposes. However, if a soul bringing a child into earth does not desire any tendency toward addictive desires, that child could come into a family where there is rampant addiction, and the child would not manifest any inherent tendency toward addictive desires.

If you look at what you would call *genetic structures*, you can see certain physiological arrangements inside a body that can produce, in some cases, over secretion of hormones, in other cases, under secretion, in other cases, over exhilarated activity in certain parts of the brain, and many different physiological responses that will establish a *tendency* to have certain kinds of feelings, certain responses to life, or certain kinds of appetites and passions.

Only in that sense could the alcoholism be considered hereditary. And, we remind you that the soul of the person would have *chosen,* before the person came into earth, those tendencies that you would call hereditary. The soul of the person would understand that tendencies toward passionate appetites, or glandular malfunctionings, or other qualities of the physiology stimulated by the soul, would be important aspects of the person's growth through the lifetime.

To believe that alcoholism or other human addictions are hereditary is as though you would put an athlete on a field, and, if he performs brilliantly, then you would say to yourself, "This must be a good field." However, if you examine this closely with your intelligence, you will realize, eventually, that the field does not make the athlete. There are other factors involved within the athlete that enable him to utilize the field with the brilliance within him. In a similar way, you need to realize that the *body* does not make the alcoholic. It is patterns within the personality and body that combine to bring about the manifestation of alcoholism.

As we have noted, certain tendencies toward patterns associated with alcoholism can be chosen by the soul of the alcoholic and placed into the personality. And, the physiology could have particular characteristics chosen by the soul that could intensify the individual's confusion, making it more likely that the person would choose to indulge in alcohol or other substances. Still, addiction is not hereditary. It is a *choice* made by the present human being. The human is also free to choose *not* to indulge. If you cannot see alcoholism and other addictions as a choice, then you cannot believe that the individual can *choose* not to indulge.

QUESTION: Is there something about our society at this point in time that is causing a tremendous amount of attention on addictions? Addictions are in the news all the time. There are many support groups. There seems to be an incredible amount of attention on addictions, and you can basically have an addiction to anything. Is it something to do with our history, particularly in the United States?

The great force that is at work here is the force of *human self indulgence*. Historically speaking, although there have always been self indulgent human beings, in the present, you ones, as a race, are becoming more and more self preoccupied, more self indulgent.

Now, this is being stimulated by a very positive inner pattern that essentially is an impulse toward *individualization*. Crudely speaking, we could say that human beings have evolved from "group" beings into individual beings, which is part of the intention of the eternal souls. However, human individuality was intended to be expressed in harmony, with the knowledge that in truth you are joined to all human beings. You are a part of them, and they are a part of you.

In the early beginnings of humanity, you ones of earth would not have had a strong sense of your own unique individuality and identity. If you would imagine yourself as an ancient human being existing during the beginning stages of human life, your inner subjective feeling as you went about your day to day living would have been: "I am this family grouping," or, "I am this tribal grouping," or, "I am this nation." You would have felt a large feeling of belonging to something bigger than yourself, as if you would feel like only one bird in a flock of birds.

As the human generations have progressed and evolved, the individual inside the human body has been more and more able to feel, "I am unique." And, as we have said, this uniqueness was intended to be celebrated and rejoiced in, in harmony with the equal realization that you are also part of all human beings. However, because of human confusion and fear, particularly in the modern period, you ones have highly developed your sense of uniqueness, but have not so clearly and strongly developed your feeling of belonging to others, of loving them, and caring for them—although many individuals *have* developed the sense of belonging and loving.

Consequently, there are many human beings in the present period who are caught up in their own experience of self. They are caught up in their own personal desires. Without enough love in their lives, without purpose and meaning, and under the influence of the habit of seeking immediate gratification, many ones, particularly in the affluent societies—even where there is poverty, pain, suffering, and depression—will lose themselves in their own desires. Because of this, whatever there is that brings immediate pleasure, they will seek it out. Many ones will overbalance toward that pleasure, and they will create a feeling that they cannot live without the drug, the food, the alcohol, the cigarette, the coffee, the exercise, or whatever it might be that brings them the pleasure. When they become so involved in their self pleasure, then they create the atmosphere for "growing" an addiction.

Human beings in the modern world, particularly in literate societies with efficient communication media, not only indulge a great deal in immediate pleasure, but, as they analyze and observe one another, they make much communication about indulgences. They begin to identify new addictions, and new ways to be self indulgent. It is this general preoccupation with self indulgence that helps propagate addictions.

QUESTION: In order to help those with a specific addiction, or those who know someone with an addiction, we would like you to address some of the specific addictions. First of all, alcohol.

Let us begin here with a feeling inside yourself. It is a feeling of extreme *sensitivity*. We would ask you to imagine this feeling as a way of identifying with those who suffer from the addiction to alcohol. To help feel this, imagine that you are in a hot bath. Your skin is extremely sensitive and alert. Suddenly, the water begins to boil. The pain of this is excruciating, because you are so sensitive, and you cannot step out of the boiling water. At all costs, you must numb your pain.

In general, most ones who choose to indulge in the alcohol, and the prolonged alcoholic stupor, will have great *emotional sensitivity*. When there is pain, it is extremely intense for them.

This is generally combined with a feeling of *impotence*. Thus, there comes, over a period of time, feelings of helplessness to be able to do anything about the pain.

Since they have not yet learned to *heal* pain, then they cannot believe that pain is temporary. They are convinced that the pain of life, primarily emotional pain, will never stop. They believe they will never be loved. They will never be safe and secure

Eventually, the pain that they feel in human life—either their own pain, or the pain of others about them—is so great, and they are so convinced that they can never heal the pain, that, in their mind, their only recourse is to *numb* the pain. Anything to numb the pain.

These are not so much their conscious thoughts. These are the unconscious patterns that drive them to seek that pleasure of numbness at all costs. They hunger for freedom from the feeling of limit and restriction that the pain imposes. Many will say that they seek the release of inhibitions, but, in reality, they seek release from their own self-created emotional pain.

In general, you could see alcohol abuse or addiction as an attempt to take *control* of life, When no other way of controlling life is found, they feel that, at least, they have the power, whenever it pleases them, to numb themselves with alcohol. They have the ability to exercise their choice and continually choose to create feelings of ''goodness'' through the use of alcohol.

Also, in lesser numbers, you will find in those of alcoholism, ones who are quite frustrated with their feelings of impotence and wish to *dominate* and *force*. You will often find violent tendencies associated with their alcohol-ism. When sober, they are terrified that they are weak, impotent, and unable to master life.

Of course, with alcohol, the brain of the physical body is affected. This causes not only a certain diminishment of physical perceptions, but it also distorts the thinking and emotional patterns. Thus, the more they drink, the more they become convinced: "There is no hope. I will never be able to heal or escape the pain of life." Then, the more they lose the little confidence they had in their ability to heal emotional pain, and to know and believe that emotional pain is temporary, the more they lose the sense that there is any goodness in life. They become blind to the extraordinary forces of love that permeate them, and all of life. They begin to despair. And the more they de-spair, the more pain they have, and the more they feel that they must have the relief of alcohol, and the numbing stupor that it brings. The more they use the alcohol, the more intense becomes the cycle of brain distortion, fol-lowed by more mental and emotional distortion. So, this is a particularly destructive addiction when carried over a period of time.

This addiction is particularly seductive for many hu-man beings in your present society. Many feel that they can "dabble" in the use of alcohol, and they can have the numbing and the thrilling feeling that they sometimes get, along with feelings of great release, without any particular risk of harm to themselves. Because of the pleasurable feelings they are preoccupied with, they do not usually notice when they slide into addiction. It is difficult for them to tell when they are simply dabbling, or when they have developed an addiction. So, it is a very difficult area for human beings, and you need to be aware of that before you dabble.

QUESTION: Would you address the addiction to drugs, such as cocaine and heroin, particularly crack cocaine that supposedly can be addictive after one or two uses?

Here, there would be some generalizable patterns, but, there are many individual reasons why human beings are led into an addiction to drugs. We will look at the general patterns.

First of all, in individuals who become addicted to drugs, there is usually an extreme self-indulgence. There might also be some of the sensitivity of the alcoholic, but, there is primarily an extremely over-exaggerated involvement with self. This would be an individual who broods on their own thoughts and feelings, and who is constantly preoccupied with their own desires, in any area, even positive areas such as growth and love. This is one who often forgets to be sensitive to others, and who is constantly obsessed with self. This is not true for all ones addicted to drugs, but does apply to many. In some, there is also the drive to numb pain.

Another general tendency is toward immediate gratification. These ones would prefer immediate inebriation rather than the slow areas attained with alcohol. They are desperate for a thrill, a fulfillment, a release.

They are usually more drastic and extreme in their personalities. They wish to entirely obliterate their pain and suffering, not slowly cover it over as the alcoholic does. They also have a tendency toward *extremes* of solutions. At times, they will tend to be violent and dramatic in their approaches to life.

Many ones addicted to drugs tend to be more private and inward drawn, whereas those who prefer the alcohol, in general, would also enjoy companionship in their alcoholic pleasures.

Beyond this, it would not suffice to generalize, for there are many individual reasons for beginning the drug addictions. With some, small numbers of them, it is simply boredom with themselves. They feel that they have no reason to be alive.

As you ones are now learning, most of the drugs have a dramatic and rapid disorienting affect upon the personality. They can quickly stimulate physical damage to tissues, particularly in the brain structure, and they can destroy certain nerve functions. In a short time, they can debilitate the physical body. So, here again, you have even stronger reasons not to dabble. It is important to try to work with your personality, to balance it, and fulfill it inwardly with your own honesty, clarity, and creativity, instead of trying to bring joy through the use of drugs.

QUESTION: What do we need to know specifically about addictions to behaviors, such as sex, exercise, or work?

The ones that we have looked at earlier who desire immediate pleasure and fulfillment from substances that impact the physical body are generally those who are more frightened, desperate, impatient, and self involved. But, those who become addicted to pleasurable experiences associated with behaviors are usually not as distorted in their personality. In the ones addicted to behaviors, there might be some self involvement, some lack of purpose and meaning, some laziness, and some of the various patterns that we have looked at earlier, but, usually it exists to a lesser degree than in those who are addicted to substances.

For example, one who you would say is addicted to sexual pleasure, unless they are extremely distorted psychologically, will generally integrate their pursuit of sexual pleasure with a relatively harmonious human life. There will be some joy in other areas. There will usually be meaningful work and relationships. But, there will also be an excessive amount of time spent in pursuing sexual pleasure. If the person is not a married person, they will usually have most of their spare time taken up with romantic relationships. If the person is married, they will usually have affairs and liaisons outside of the marriage, which, of course, will create peripheral challenges and complexify their life.

Ordinarily, unless there is psychological distortion in the person, there will not be physically damaging results from addictions to behaviors. If you are addicted to exercise because of the thrill and pleasure you receive from it emotionally, mentally, and physically—which is related to glandular responses in your physical body—unless you are unintelligent and go too far in your exercise, you will not damage your body. You will simply spend a great deal of time exercising.

In the area of addiction to behaviors, as long as you are not extremely overbalanced, you might say that you could rejoice that you have found something so meaningful in your life. However, you need to be alert to the fact that when you become obsessed with one area of behavior, then it has gone beyond meaningful activity, and it is robbing the other activities in your life that could also be very important and meaningful to you.

For example, let us say that it is very important for a certain female one to have a marriage and family. It is important from her personality point of view, and from her soul's point of view. But, even though she marries and begins a family, because of certain fears of loneliness, and fears that she is unworthy, she begins to desire that male ones other than her marriage one will love her.

Since she is quite passionate and sexual, in order to create love, she begins to flirt with and seduce male ones. She begins to create affairs and liaisons.

Then, these areas become so immediately pleasurable to her that she does not give enough attention to her relationship with her husband and family. In fact, she begins to create a feeling that says, "My husband and family are boring. Liaisons and sexual relationships outside of the marriage are exciting and stimulating." As these feelings grow more extreme, she feels that she must have the freedom to indulge herself in the more exciting area, and she convinces herself that marriage and family are unimportant.

Now, because it was truly her personality and soul's desire to have the fulfillments of marriage and family, we could say that her addiction to affairs is not beneficial to her. It is not bad. It is not evil. It is simply not what she truly desired in her life. She is free to engage in the other liaisons, but they will eventually bring challenge and confusion, and, at some point, she will need to see her fears that drove her to be addicted to affairs, and she will need to heal those fears.

In your human definitions, you may wish to see an "addiction" to behavior as an area in which one part of the personality feels that it cannot live without a certain experience, while another part feels that it does not wish to engage in that experience. You might say that it is a "compulsion" that the calmer, larger part of the personality does not truly desire, but the smaller, impatient, impulsive, frightened part of the personality feels it cannot live without.

In such cases, the individual would have built a strong feeling that *ordinary human experience* is very empty, lacking in joy, in purpose and meaning. They feel that ordinary experience it too boring, frustrating, sad, or painful. Daily life seems extremely negative in different ways.

Then, for many reasons that have to do with environment, examples from society and family, and factors in the personality, such an individual will begin an activity that stands out against the background of boredom and meaninglessness. That activity might stand out as the only joyful thing to do in life. The only way to feel a stirring of positive intensity.

Usually these areas will begin quite minimally. In other words, if the one goes to do gambling, it simply gives a slight upliftment. But, feeling that there is no other possibility of uplifting in life, the one will return to that slight stirring experience and do it again. Then, as this new experience stands out in contrast to the flatness of the rest of the life, all of the intensity of feeling that is being blocked and prevented from flowing into *all* areas of life, in a quite distorted way, is turned toward this one particular area. This area becomes the "scapegoat" for the entire life.

This is particularly likely to happen in areas such as sexual fulfillment, and other areas that have an inherent intensity. Such areas can become so important, by contrast to the flatness of the rest of life, that gradually, the distorted feelings are exaggerated until there is a belief that says: "There can be no joy in life unless I am doing this activity."

The healing of these areas involves turning intensity and passion back toward the areas of life that seem so flat, boring, frustrating, painful, or frightening. The passion needs to be redistributed throughout all areas of life so that it is not all collected in one area. Most ones will approach the healing of addictive and compulsive behaviors by trying to *prohibit* the behavior. For some, this is necessary. However, for most, it is easier to "redistribute" the passions by *reducing the contrast between the compulsive behavior and the ordinary life.*

It is beneficial to see this as though you have put all

eggs in one basket. Now you wish to spread them among many baskets. So, there is a need to train the personality to seize upon that feeling of heightened intensity and greater passion that is stirred in the obsessive area, and gently begin to transfer it, by creativity, by interest, by curiosity, into other areas. It is easier to do this with areas that are inherently fascinating, such as human relationships, artistic activity, or meaningful giving to other human beings.

In general, what you ones have labeled as addictions to certain behaviors are more manageable than addictions to substances. Essentially, the healing of addictive behaviors is a matter of *retraining a frightened personality*. The addictions to behaviors grow over a longer period of time, so they are usually not so intense. With the proper counseling and inner work, the deep desires involved in those addictions can usually be fulfilled in broader ways. The extreme behaviors can be balanced and harmonized, and the life can be re-stimulated to become more evenly balanced across many different human experiences.

In general, it is a wise way to guide yourself to say: "If I have narrowed my life to the point that only one experience is fulfilling for me, then I have some work to do. I have come into this lifetime to rejoice in an entire range of experiences—the physical pleasures, the intellectual stimulations, the emotional fulfillments, the joy of the spiritual experience." In a sense, a large goal in your life is to fulfill in all of those areas simultaneously.

QUESTION: Eating disorders, such as bulimia and anorexia have become more prevalent in the past dec-

ade—bulimia being essentially an addiction to bingeing and purging, and anorexia an addiction to not eating at all. What can you tell us about these food related addictive behaviors?

There are many areas to look at here. Again, some are individual and apply only to certain ones, and some are generalizable. There are some who enter into this area as a kind of superficial "trick." They would say, "I desire to be thin, and I will regurgitate my food," in ignorance of the potentially severe consequences. Or, they would say, "I will simply not eat." In such ones, there are not necessarily deep psychological disturbances. They simply play with this trick, this activity, and, gradually, they become addicted to the ease of it, and to the pleasure of it.

More common are the ones with deep, disturbing patterns within their personality that would have to do with *self diminishment*, feelings of *unworthiness*, and *overcriticalness* toward themselves. These patterns are usually stimulated by a harsh parent in the early stages of their life. This is not always the case, but many times the child will internalize harsh, critical tendencies displayed toward them in childhood by family members. And, usually, in this food disorder area, which, as you can observe, often manifests in female ones, much of the self condemnation will center upon the lack of physical beauty of the body. Of course, they will be particularly sensitive to obesity.

For many of these ones, there is often a past lifetime on earth in which they have been quite obese, and they have suffered emotionally from it, either through the ridicule of others, or from the loss of a love relationship.

For some, there has been early obesity in the present life-time. In either case, the harsh criticalness that they adopt toward themselves can push them to do anything to avoid being obese and "ugly" in their own eyes. The ones who engage in the eating disorders from this impulse have a great deal to heal within themselves.

Over a period of time, the eating disorder, just as with the addiction to substances, will alter the chemistry of the body. It will begin to affect the brain itself, as well as the tissues, cells, blood, and nerves of the body. This will distort the judgment, and the thinking and emotional patterns, usually pushing the individual toward *extremism.* This distortion can even stir up mental illness in the most extreme cases. Such chemical distortion makes it even more difficult for the individual to understand what they are doing in their eating habits. It will be more difficult to grapple with the underlying harsh self criticism and condemnation of their physical beauty, and all of the underlying causes of their addiction.

In the area of eating disorders, the first challenge is to convince the personality to restrain from abusing the food, whether they are avoiding eating food, or whether they are regurgitating it. This can be very difficult, as you may have observed.

After there has been some headway made in at least partially controlling the abnormal behavior toward food, then the individual must work diligently to bring the underlying sense of self hatred, self diminishment, or self criticalness to the surface. Those negative feelings need to be experienced and healed.

Then, they must work to bring their fears to the surface and heal them. The fear that they are unlovable. The fear of being rejected and harshly criticized. Some even have fears of being punished and damaged if they are not perfectly beautiful and perfectly acceptable to others.

In these areas, there is layer upon layer of complexity within the personality patterns. Often, it takes a great deal of therapeutic intervention and assistance to help such individuals, particularly those who have been engaged in their addictive practice for a long period of time.

So, in communicating about addictive behaviors with food, there needs to be alertness and caution, particularly with youthful ones. You will need to show them that some of these habits can, in time, be as potentially destructive as putting drugs into the body. And, you would show them that it is certainly not an intelligent choice to dabble in these behaviors.

QUESTION: Would you speak to the loved ones who have to stand by while perhaps a child, or a relative grapples with an addiction? Many times that loved one feels impotent and guilty, and they have difficulty in determining how much they are going to enable the person, or stand firm with them. What would you say to the loved ones?

First of all, in trying to understand a loved one with an addiction, you would say to yourself: "The deepest thread of challenge in their addiction is usually a lack of joy, and a diminished sense of purpose and meaning." When your actions cause them *less* joy, cause them to feel *less* purpose and meaning, then those actions will not usually be beneficial. When you can find actions, and ways of communicating, that help them feel *more* joyful about life, and give them *more* purpose and meaning, then, in general, that might be helpful.

It might be helpful if you could say to one who is a loved one to you in that situation, "I so need you to help me learn how to work with you now." You can try to find small ways to show them how important they are to you. Ask them to help you with simple activities, and to be with you as you do things. It is also very important to try to find ways to communicate your love for them.

Eventually, depending upon the relationship and the situation, it might be necessary to communicate your fears to them. Instead of trying to force them to do what you believe they need to do to heal their addiction, or solve their challenge, usually you will need to begin by saying: "I love you so much, and I am so frightened for your well being. Are you willing to talk to me about my fears?" As you do this, try not to blame them and accuse them, for usually they are accusing themselves quite viciously and energetically. They do not need your help in accusing themselves.

At times, depending upon the situation, you may need to love them from a distance. In other words, there may be such distortion in their thinking and feeling that they simply cannot communicate with you. And, at times, trying to communicate will exacerbate the situation. At such times, your only reasonable choice is to love them from a distance. You will need to try and trust that they are eternal souls, and even if the addictive behavior eventually destroys their body and sends it to death, it will not damage their eternal being. This is a very difficult thing to accomplish, and each one will need to work with the individual factors in their loved one, and in themselves, in order to know when this approach is necessary.

Generally, it is very beneficial to have help in working with a loved one who has an addiction. It is not wise to try to work alone. Surround yourself with ones who can encourage you and love you, particularly ones who are familiar with the challenges. Accept help and guidance from others so that you do not feel that you are battling alone.

Of course, the greatest gift to the one you are working with is your *love*. Whenever you feel love toward the one who is struggling, and you sense that they are willing to receive expressions of it, try to say the love, try to express it in any way that you can. Hopefully, the love will penetrate their confused patterns and convince them that one important purpose in their life is the love that you are sharing with them.

QUESTION: For someone caught up in an addiction, it is very difficult to resist the addictive desires. Would you give us a method to use in an emergency addiction situation when we feel like we just can't go on without having the thing that we are addicted to?

First of all, you would say to yourself, "This desire has been *created* by me." No matter what you are addicted to, even if it has distorted your thoughts and your feelings, even if scientifically you would believe that you have a chemical dependence, the desire for the addictive pleasure has been created by you. Therefore, you must convince yourself that you have the power to *change* that desire. This can be difficult, but it is a starting point for your work.

Next, you would say to yourself, "This feeling that I have, the feeling that I cannot live without the experience that I get from my addictive area, is only a *feeling*. It is a feeling that lives inside me. It is *created* by me. I have the power to *change* that feeling."

Next, you would say, "The reason that I am so desperate for the experience of the addiction is that there has not been enough joy and love in my life, and I am afraid that there never will be. In this moment, if only I could find some joy and love, then I could substitute the pleasure of joy and love for the pleasure that I expect to get from this addiction."

These ways of working provide a starting point. If you cannot control your desires by working with these kinds of inner thoughts and feelings, then you need the help of other human beings. Seek out counseling ones, particularly those who have, in their own lives, successfully healed the addiction that you are struggling with.

For some, if the addiction is not chemical, or obsessive, or overpowering, it can be beneficial to remind yourself: You did not come into this lifetime to indulge in your own pleasures. You came to express the beauty of God by loving other human beings, and by giving to them. Your own personal fulfillment is important, but it is only half of the equation of life. And, if you continue the self indulgence of the addictive behavior, most likely, you are not going to fulfill your purpose in this lifetime of giving to others, loving them, helping them.

However, you would not need to be afraid that it is bad to be self indulgent. You have eternity to continue to try to perfect your human expression. If you become lost in your self indulgence, then you will simply come into a future lifetime with the same challenge of obsessiveness with your own desires and your own pleasure. Instead of fully extending beauty and love into that future lifetime, instead of extending the true joy, the true fulfillment, which is so extraordinary, but often feels so subtle and elusive, you would extend the struggle with self indulgence.

The true joy and fulfillment of life is *love*—love of yourself, of other human beings, and of God. But, it takes time and effort to fully penetrate the intensity of experiences of love. When you feel trapped by your own addictive desire, you could say to yourself: "If I, in this moment, continue to fulfill this self indulgent desire through my addictive behavior, I only put off the time when I can penetrate the extraordinary fulfillments of love. I push that time further into the future. And, it will seem more and more difficult to attain those experiences of love. I will have a difficult time believing that it is even possible to fulfill myself in love."

It would be important to try to take this approach without frightening yourself. There is no badness in an entire lifetime of addiction. There is only pain and suffering.

There can also be the loss of those extraordinary experiences of love, and purpose and meaning that are your intended fulfillment in this lifetime. When you lose yourself in an addiction, it is as though you would say, "I love to eat dirt," and you eat so much dirt that you do not have time to eat the wonderful feast that has been spread on the table before you. That is not a thing to be frightened of, but you need to be quite clear about the seriousness of your choice. When you fill your human experience with the addictive experience, you temporarily crowd out those most important experiences of love that are your true purpose in this lifetime. And, you more and more convince yourself that you cannot fulfill those true purposes. You must settle for only the immediate pleasure of the addiction. You convince yourself: "I cannot have the feast. I must eat dirt for the rest of this lifetime."

QUESTION: Would you give us an ongoing way to work to heal our addictions?

Each morning, as you arise, you need to focus your attention on the *truth*. No matter what your immediate thoughts or feelings might be, even if you arise feeling, "I am so depressed, life is without meaning, there is no purpose for me," before you begin to indulge in those kinds of distorted patterns, you need to remind yourself of the truth. To help accomplish this, as soon as your eyes are open each morning, whether you can believe it or not, say to yourself:

"The purpose of my life is to express the magnificent forces of God itself through my human

thinking, feeling, acting, and doing. Perhaps I seem to be far from that. So be it. As long as I know that this is my purpose, and in this day I do my best to move toward it, then I am doing well."

It does not matter whether in your distortion you see yourself as the hopeless alcoholic, the "dope fiend," the obese "pig" stuffing yourself with food—no matter how negative your attitude toward yourself might be, and no matter how long you have had it—as long as you are willing to try to begin your day by reminding yourself of your true purpose, and as long as you are willing to try, to the best of your ability, to live that purpose according to what you believe is the perfect way to live it, then, you can say to yourself, "I have reason to rejoice in me, even if I feel that I am a horrible addict." This kind of inner work done day by day will begin to drive a wedge into your habits of addiction. It will begin to make a small place within your confused patterns where you can feel that you are truly a valuable human being. No matter how bad you may come to feel about yourself in your distortion, the truth is that *you are an expression of God in human form.*

In other words, when you are struggling with addictive desires, you must begin to carve out a small place in your feelings where you convince yourself that you are a magnificent human being. You are not bad, or wrong, or unworthy simply because you are struggling with an addictive desire. It will be very difficult to heal addictive desires unless you feed yourself each day with a feeling of your own goodness, your own worthiness.

So, begin each day by insisting upon celebrating you, whether your thoughts and feelings can believe in your goodness or not. You must take the time to feed the truth into your own mind. You would say to yourself each day:

"I am an expression of God in human form. I have many magnificent qualities. To the best of my ability, I will try to express those qualities in this day."

Next, try to plan what you will do each day to draw your attention away from yourself. This is necessary in order to adjust your tendency toward self preoccupation. The most effective way to do this is to look about at the human beings around you, at the ones in need. What can you do to help them? It does not need to be a large, dramatic thing that you do. You might say, "My friend is sad. I will go to her. I will embrace her, and encourage her." Or, you might say, "This child needs some care while the parents go on a journey. I will offer myself." The more that you turn your attention to others, the faster you will heal, for you will break that hypnotic cycle of self preoccupation and self indulgence.

Also, the more you can feel your eternal nature, the more you will heal. It is very important to feel that you are much more than an addicted human being. You need to feel that beneath your personality challenges, you are an eternal soul. As an eternal soul, you have extraordinary resources to draw upon. You have much more strength, courage, and wisdom than you are aware of. You will need to learn to believe in deeper, larger forces than you

are usually aware of. You must try to know that those
forces live inside you. They are the *truth* of you. Your
addictive desires are *temporary*. The forces of love within
you are *permanent*.

Again, we would remind you that if your addictive desires and behaviors are very strong, you will need the help
of other human beings in your healing. You will need the
counseling ones. You will need the help of the friends and
loved ones who are around you. You will need to communicate with them as you work on healing your addictive
patterns.

You will also need to heal your pain and suffering by
bringing it to the surface. You will need to talk about
your inner negativity, learning that it is only *thoughts* and
feelings. Negative thoughts and feelings are *temporary*.
You can heal them.

So, day after day, you can work in these ways, and
you will eventually heal anything that troubles you.

For the moment, imagine that you are being surrounded with warmth and joy. Give yourself now to a
moment of silence. In the silence, begin to feel, inside
you, a love that is very strong. Let yourself feel this
strong love that is so much more than human emotion. It
is a *force*, a *power*.

Begin to feel now that the force of this love is so strong
that nothing that you think, or feel, or do in this lifetime
can diminish it. You can ignore this love. You can avoid
it. You can refuse to believe in it. But, it continues to
pour forth into your heart, constantly. It is the force of

God itself. And this love would never condemn you—not for your addiction, nor for your challenges. It would *always* continue to love you, and encourage you to heal.

In this moment, and in future moments, try to feel:

This love will never abandon you. This love will never reject you because you *appear* to be less than perfect. This love will guide you, and sustain you, *always*.

Whenever you are willing to take a moment of silence and put aside your self condemnation, your self preoccupation, and your turmoils, you can feel this love soothing you, guiding you, comforting you.

So, feel it in this moment. Give yourself to it. And rejoice in it.

Chapter Six

HEALING THE HURT CHILD

Resolving the Pain of Childhood

Many adults in your present society have emotional wounds that are related to suffering that they have endured in childhood. And, we could say that within those adults who have known deep pain and suffering in their growing years, there is a "hurt child."

Those adults who have a hurt child within them will often stir up an unconscious tendency to draw toward other human beings who have the potential to help them stimulate a healing process. So, as we begin with you an understanding of the pain of childhood, the healing of it, and the reasons why adults inflict pain upon children, we suggest that you start with the willingness to believe that the adults who presently struggle with the experience of having been abused as children, will tend to intuitively draw toward ones who can help them in their present day to day life.

This is a generalization that can be helpful to you if you are one of those who has suffered abuse as a child. You could begin to look at the ones presently in your life, and you could say, "If I am tending to draw near to ones who now help me heal, then what role does this person play? What role can that one play?" This is simply to suggest that you be alert to identify ones around you who can be of service to you in your healing process.

Now, as we look closer at the area of the abuse of children, and its consequences, we must gently remind you that this present lifetime is one of *many* human lifetimes that you have lived. At this point in time, you are a culmination of many things that you have been as a human being in the past. And, whether you have suffered child abuse in this lifetime or not, we remind you that you have been a human child many times, and most of you have had some extremely painful human childhood experiences *before* your present lifetime. So, if you are struggling with pain and suffering in this lifetime from your childhood experiences, you can use this thought as a reminder to yourself that you have suffered in other lifetimes when you were a child, and, *the suffering has not diminished or damaged your being.* It was painful when you were alive in the past, but, in each lifetime, you would make your death, and, after a period of human time after your death, you would make adjustments so that the pain and suffering would no longer exist.

This is a valuable knowing to hold in your mind and in your heart as you approach your all important *present* lifetime. Even though knowledge of your past lifetimes can be helpful, you are living in the present, and your present life needs most of your attention. If you are one who has been "abused" as a child in this lifetime, there are many ways to approach that fact in the present. And we will explore those ways with you. We will help you understand yourself, both as a child, and as an adult in the present.

We will also help you deepen your sense of yourself as an *eternal being* who eventually will make death in *this* lifetime, and will put behind you all pain and suffering that you have experienced in this lifetime. But, between your birth in this lifetime and your death, there are many human experiences that you are having that are very important to you, and to the human beings about you in your life. Those human experiences are also important to your own *soul*. For, in a way, the human experiences that you have on earth in this lifetime feed into the extraordinary vastness of yourself as an eternal soul. So, not only are you working to fulfill your human personality in your life, but you are also feeding your eternal soul by your present experiences in earth life.

However, as you live your human life, you need to understand that your soul does not fall into despair if you feed it painful experiences. As a human being, you can fall into despair when you are in pain. But, your soul has a larger vision of that experience. Your soul understands that pain is *temporary*, that it is *human*. So, you could say to yourself:

> "I live for myself as a human being. But I also feed into my soul all that I live in this lifetime. It is not *bad* when I have pain and negative experience. It *feels* bad to me as a human, but it is not a badness in life."

Next, you could say to yourself:

> "The more healing that I can do, the more joyful this lifetime will be for me. That will please *me* deeply. It will also feed joy into my soul, and it will please my soul. But, I remind myself that my soul is not *displeased* when I am having challenging experiences as a human being."

It is of great importance to fully engage all of your human experience in this lifetime. If you are one who has been abused as a child, you need to give that some attention, to make some understanding, and growing, and healing. And, in your healing work with your important *human* experience, it can help you to say to yourself: "I am an eternal being." When you feel overcome, or overwhelmed, or frustrated, or lost, or limited by some of your challenging experiences, memories, thoughts, or feelings, you can gently remind yourself:

> "These challenging areas are *temporary*. I will eventually heal them. I am drawing upon my eternal nature to do so. I am drawing upon that which is much larger than my human capacities. I

am drawing upon divine forces to help me in my healing."

These are some ways to expand your thoughts and feelings to create some larger attitudes as you approach your work with the actual experience, or memory of the painful childhood. These can also be beneficial if you are one who is helping another person to heal. These kinds of thoughts and feelings can help you in any healing work.

QUESTION: Child abuse is widespread these days. It is said that one in three women, and one in seven men, will be sexually abused in childhood. What is it in our society that is propagating such behavior?

As we look with you now at factors that stir within many people, and that are related to the sexual abuse of children, we will look first at the societal factors, then we will look at the impact upon the individuals who make the abuse, particularly the male individuals.

In the present society of your United States, and this applies to a lesser degree to some other societies on the earth, there is, first of all, in many people, *a great fear that you will not be complete in this lifetime.* You ones have so inundated yourselves with knowledge of catastrophe, disaster, pain, suffering, violent death, and war, and all of those quite horrible human experiences have so saturated your consciousness through your images of the television, the filmings, and so forth, that there has grown a widespread sense within many that says, "I can never be fulfilled. One of these dangerous and terrible things in life will eventually destroy me.''

This goes hand in hand with a certain tendency that is stimulated by your societal communications that is, *an impatience to have your desires fulfilled*. Your communication media teach you, through advertising and so forth, that it is wonderful to have passionate desires, and to fulfill them immediately.

So, the impatience, the passion for immediate gratification, and the focus upon disaster that causes you to feel, ''One of these horrible things in life will eat me, swallow me, and destroy me,'' all combine to cause many to feel, ''There is not much time before one of these disasters befalls me, and I need immediate gratification. There is no reason to *restrain* myself.''

These forces, combined with a certain tendency to be *preoccupied with self*, to lose yourself in the intensity of your own thoughts, feelings, and desires, all combine with a kind of attitude toward sexual fulfillment that is quite widespread in the present period—the attitude that sexual pleasure is simply a sound, healthy activity that is quite equal to any other pleasure. In past generations in your country, when this sexual attitude was not so prevalent, there was child abuse, but, now, many ones, particularly male ones, who are confused, under the pressures of these societal influences, will take the attitude: ''I must have my sexual fulfillment. That is all that is important. And sexual fulfillment is almost like a sport. It is quite legitimate. It is quite good.''

Such attitudes are reinforced by the fact that there are whole industries in your country built upon sexual fulfillment. Many things encourage a feeling that whatever the sexual desire in a male one might be, it is good for them to follow it. And, if such ones happen to have a desire to have sexual intercourse with a child, or, to make some kind of sexual liaison with a child, the part of that person's personality that would normally say: "But, what would this do to the child? What are my concerns for the child?" that part of the person tends to be *numbed*. It is numbed by their over-focus upon immediate gratification, the fear of life being negative and painful, and the over-emphasis upon sexual fulfillment. All of these combine to cause the individual to become lost in their own desires and impulses, and to swallow the aspect of themselves that could be sensitive to another human being, that could be aware of how frightening and painful it would be for a child to be sexually abused.

These are some of the *generalizable* patterns in those who would abuse children. Individuals, of course, will have their own unique personal patterns. Some will have a sense of shame and terribleness from the way they themselves were sexually abused as children. This will cause some psychological disturbances of a rather unique nature.

There are many personal factors involved in those who abuse children. But, they will usually combine with the general factors that we have mentioned, and together, these factors lead one to be carried away by sexual desire, and to ignore the human sensitivities that ordinarily they would have toward the impact of their actions upon their "victim."

In your society, the influences upon male ones are generally different than upon females. And, in general, as you can observe, those who choose to express in earth in the male human form usually have more interest in sexual fulfillment. They also, speaking generally, have less restraint and patience, in terms of responding to strong sexual desires. As a generalization, we could say that most male ones are not as interested in feelings and sensitive areas as are the females. So, many male ones will allow themselves to be overpowered by sexual desires, and they will often allow those desires to override their ideals, their morals, and their sensitivities.

When you need a sense in your own mind of what are some broad, general causes of child abuse, these areas that we have mentioned can be a starting point for you. However, it is wise to treat each instance in your experience as an individual event, looking for the unique understandings for that particular situation.

QUESTION: The incidence of *emotional* child abuse—meaning that parents or others are constantly cruel, or verbally degrade children—has not been calculated. What is it that would cause parents to emotionally abuse their own child?

There are several generalizable patterns here. The largest, in both male and female, is the sense of *badness* that they feel about themselves. If you are a mother or father, and you feel inside yourself, "I am such a terrible person, I am bad," then, when you see an action by the child that displeases you, you respond in an exaggerated, distorted way because you feel, "This thing that my child has done is *bad*." You over-respond and feel that the child itself is bad. You become frightened that if you do not put up a countering force to make the child be different, then the child will be quite horrible, and your life will be horrible. Most of this is done in an unconscious way. You are not usually aware of these underlying factors.

For many who have these kind of patterns, there is often an influence from pain and suffering that they have experienced in their own childhood. There was not enough love and gentleness for them.

When a father or mother feels, "I am terrible, I am bad," they create such feelings of inadequacy within themselves that they are quite unhappy in their own lives. This causes much fear, which can cause them to become quite angry at their children. Under the influence of the anger, they can even begin to feel, "There is badness in this child. This child is a threat, or even an enemy." Then, the more badness they believe they see in the child, the more forceful they believe they must be to oppose the child. At times, they can actually create feelings of *hatred* for their own child. Usually, this is temporary. It mixes with love that they might have. But, they become so overwhelmed by their own negative patterns that they lose sight of the beauty, the goodness, and the magnificence that lives in the child. Since they have lost the capacity to see that goodness in themselves, they have difficulty seeing it in their child.

When parents become caught up in their own intense negative patterns of thinking and feeling, they temporarily lose their ability to be sensitive to, and to understand their children. They also lose sight of the impact of their behavior on their children. So, in those moments in which they are emotionally abusing the child, they lose sight of the child entirely. In such moments, they do not even care about the result of their negative behaviors upon the child. Because they are so caught up in all of the tumultuous negativity inside themselves, they are not capable of looking to see the consequences of their actions.

Now, what is so difficult for the adult who has had the experience of being emotionally abused as a child by the father or mother, is the conviction that the father or mother did not love them. This is an understandable response. But, in truth, the love is usually there. However, is was temporarily overwhelmed by the fear and the negativity of the father or mother.

These are very difficult areas, so you will need to be patient in understanding them. The more you condemn the fathers and mothers who emotionally abuse their children, the more you intensify their fears and their negative feelings, and the more likely they are to exaggerate their abuse of children. The key, of course, is a difficult, but very important process of *education*, *enlightenment*, and *healing* of the fathers and mothers in their own personalities.

QUESTION: How would you characterize the difference in the effects of sexual child abuse versus emotional child abuse?

Here, there are many unique factors that are not generalizable, but, in general, the sexual abuse comes forth as a kind of *detached* activity, on the part of the perpetrator. In other words, the one who sexually abuses the child is detached from their deeper, truer feelings. During the sexual abuse, they will generally be emotionally detached from the child, so they will tend to use the child as an *object* for their own pleasure.

Often, the result of this behavior inflicted upon a child will be that in the child's adulthood, they will tend to feel that there is no depth, or warmth, or love in life. They will also have a tendency to numb themselves emotionally. This habit of emotional detachment is caused in their childhood by a blind groping for anything to inwardly protect themselves while they are being abused. In their confusion, pain, and suffering as children, they will search for something inwardly that will help them, and they usually end up learning not to feel, in order to block out the painful feelings. This emotional detachment is intensified by the tendency of the sexual abuser to detach and be isolated.

When abused children become adults, because of their need not to feel pain, they will often have strong habits of emotional numbing. In order to heal, they will need to struggle to open their emotions and feel deeply. In particular, they will need to learn how to feel and work with *painful* emotions. This will lead, in time, to an opening to positive, loving feelings.

Those are some predominant, generalizable areas for children who are sexually abused.

For those children who are emotionally abused, who are constantly derided, condemned, criticized, and treated harshly and angrily, when they become an adult, they will usually have a passionate *anger*, and other strong feelings. They will be deeply interested in all feelings, and will need to feel strong emotions. Even though they will usually be frightened of feeling condemned or criticized, they will tend to be fascinated by such feelings. They will also tend to be emotionally *needy* for positive, loving feelings, and for approval from others.

Such adults might have a tendency to numb themselves emotionally, because they have had such pain from emotional abuse as a child. But, they will tend to be extremely sensitive emotionally, so they can have a hunger for strong feelings, even when they are trying to emotionally detach.

Most of these adults will not like negative feelings, but some of them may develop what you might call a "masochistic" tendency. They will unconsciously associate painful emotions with sexual pleasure, or love, because, in their childhood, pain became mixed in with their love for the abusing parent.

In general, the most common manifestation in adults who have been emotionally abused as children will be the *emotional neediness*. They will be deeply feeling adults who are hungry for approval, warmth, love, and inclusion. And, of course, there are many other *individual* effects, so each case must be seen in its own unique way.

QUESTION: Would you outline the steps that are crucial for an individual to heal the effects of childhood sexual abuse?

Let us suggest that the first step is *the experiencing of and venting* of emotional pain and suffering, negative thoughts and feelings, and fears. There can be a tendency to feel, "In order to heal, I must *eliminate* my negative memories, painful emotions, thoughts, and present fears." They will feel that their inner negativity in the present is the problem. They will feel, "I was abused, but now my problem is all of this negativity inside me." Many will become frantic to eliminate the negativity, to push it away, to try to do something very strong and forceful so that they do not need to have their negative inner experiences. This often leads to a swallowing, suppressing, or hiding of their fears, and their negative thoughts, feelings, and memories.

This swallowing of negativity causes the negativity to "fester," so to speak. The negative inner patterns accumulate as negative "energies" within the personality. These negative energies can eventually warp the personality. At times, they can even cause some challenges to the health of the physical body.

So, in the healing, first of all, it is very important for the individuals to *live through* and *fully experience* the negativity associated with the childhood abuse. They will need to explore the memories, the thoughts, the feelings, the fears, and the doubts about themselves in the present.

Then, for the *venting* of negativity, it will be very important to *share* these feelings, thoughts, memories, and so forth. They need to speak them out loud to another human being who is loving, understanding, and patient—one they can trust. The healing could *possibly* be done alone, but it is more difficult, and more confusing.

After you work to experience and vent your inner thoughts, feelings, memories, fears, and so forth, the next challenge is to convince the frightened child in you that no matter how horrible the experience of abuse was, it is in the *past*. And, if you are not presently being abused, then you are not in danger, you are not diminished, or damaged. You can begin to try to feel:

> **"These thoughts, feelings, memories, and fears are painful, but, what I am learning as I explore them, live them without resistance, share them, and work with them, is that they are *only* thoughts, feelings, and memories. *They cannot damage me.*"**

The *feelings* that you might have that say, "This is *bad* that I have been sexually abused, I am ruined, I am diminished, I am in danger," are important feelings to recognize and to work with. But, as you do your healing, eventually, you will come to the point where you realize:

> **"These are *feelings*. They may have been painful and frightening, but they are not the *truth* about me. I *feel* that I am damaged, but, in truth, I am not. I *feel* that it is very bad that I have had this experience, but that is a temporary *feeling,* an emotion. It is not a permanent truth about my being."**

The next step is a kind of rebuilding of the *vision of self*, the *feelings about yourself.* This goes hand in hand with, and extends the process of convincing yourself that you are not diminished, dirtied, ruined, or damaged. You begin the rebuilding by simply accepting, bit by bit, the *truth.* The truth can be said to yourself in this simple way, with as much feeling as possible:

"I am not damaged in my being."

The next step is to *extend* the true vision of yourself, so that you can see, not only are you not damaged, but you are quite *magnificent* as a human being. All of the goodness, creativity, and wonderful abilities in you have not been eliminated because you were sexually abused as a child. That experience might make it more difficult for you to *feel* your magnificence, but it cannot *eliminate* it.

In this stage, the task—and it can be a difficult one, perhaps taking a long period of time—is to convince the child in you that you still have magnificent qualities as a part of your being. The frightened, damaged-feeling part of you needs to feel that your magnificence has not been lost. You have creativity, you have beauty, you have goodness, you have worthiness within your being.

This leads to the next step. which is, *convincing yourself that you are also extremely lovable, and you have a very deep capacity to love others.* It is understandable that if you have suffered sexual abuse, at times you will feel, "Others cannot love me. I cannot love them fully. I am stunted in my ability to love." No matter how strong these feelings are, you work to remind yourself, they are only *feelings.* They are not the truth about your being. No matter how frightened you may have been as a result of the abuse, you need to remind yourself that it is only *fear*, and you must experience it, live through it, and heal it.

The feelings in you that say that you are not lovable,

that you cannot love others, are *temporary emotions. Your capacity to love and be loved is permanent.* It can never be diminished. You can become frightened and fear to use this capacity. You can become confused and believe you have no capacity to love, *feeling* that you can only hate and resent. But, hatred and resentment are also feelings. They are temporary. *Your capacity to love and be loved is permanent.* It lives inside you. It can never can be lost. You can only ignore it, or fail to believe in it.

As you work to gain the vision of your true, magnificent self, it will eventually lead to a conviction that your ability to love and be loved has not been diminished by the experience of abuse. Even though, in your human confusion, you may not feel *perfectly* healed, as you work to heal your inner negativity, you will convince yourself:

"I can love deeply and fully throughout this lifetime, and others can love me."

The next step is to gently study your *behaviors* with other human beings, especially in romantic and sexual areas. You will need to be very loving with yourself in this study, for you might have developed some rather bizarre habits of behavior from your painful experiences of abuse, and from your distorted responses to those experiences. So, be patient with any difficult patterns that you discover within yourself.

In this study of your behaviors, it is important to work with ones you trust. Say to them, "I am trying to open my heart and use my full ability to love. Will you help me? Will you listen while I talk about some difficult behavior patterns that I have discovered within my personality. Listen while I talk about the tightness, tension, and fear that I feel when it is time to open emotionally.''

Not only is it beneficial to communicate with others in this way, but you can ask them to help you practice adjusting your behaviors. In other words, you practice changing the behaviors that you learn are clearly linked to your past pain and distortion. You strive to stir new behaviors that are linked to your new vision of yourself, your new trust, your new love.

The final step in your healing is, *regaining a sense of beauty and love in sharing yourself intimately with another person*. You will teach yourself that the sexual expression can be linked with idealism, gentleness, goodness, and love. For some, this can be the most difficult part of the healing. And, many may go to their death in this lifetime not feeling *perfect* about sexual expression. Yet, they will make wonderful, extraordinary healings in the emotional areas. They will be extremely loving and receptive, deeply giving, and very joyful.

Even though we have described a direction that you might say is a movement toward perfect healing, if you occasionally have feelings of being imperfectly healed, you must gently remind yourself, that too is a *feeling*. Work with that feeling and heal it.

You need to be very patient with the hurt child within you. Always taking a loving, gentle approach. If you try a thing and you seem to fail, say to yourself, ''I am disappointed that I failed. But I rejoice that I tried. And I can *always* try. Eventually, I will make the changes that will please me, and fulfill me.''

You will totally heal some challenges in your present lifetime. Rejoice in that, even if they seem to be few in number. Many of you can heal most of your human challenges in this lifetime, with only a few threads of remaining challenge that you will take into your death. The unhealed challenges will not damage your being. They will not be a failing in this lifetime. It is difficult for human beings to create full perfection in any area, because you are so complex, and you embody such a range of thoughts and feelings, from the deeply negative, to the magnificently positive.

QUESTION: How can the mate of a victim of child abuse best help that person in the healing process?

Here is a very important area. If you have been abused as a child, and you do all that we have suggested, and you make a mating relationship with one who is afraid to open their heart and give to you fully, nurture you, and love you, then you may still have deep pain and challenges, even though you have done everything perfectly within yourself. If you wish to heal *alone*, you can do it all by yourself. But, if you wish to heal and also love and be loved in a mating or marriage, then, of course, much depends upon the one you love.

If you are the one that the abused one loves—the mate, the friend, or a loved one of any kind to an adult who is healing the effects of child abuse—the first and most important guiding principle for you is, *patience*. You must strive not to become desperate or frantic to rush the healing process. It can be painful to watch your loved one struggle through certain areas of the healing. It is natural for you to feel, "I must do something quickly, for my beloved one is in pain." You will need to be patient in order to remember that it is their healing, not yours. If you would say, "I must heal them," then you rob them. You overpower them. You dominate them.

The second important quality is *sensitivity*. Even though it may be painful for you to be near them as they suffer, you will need to have the courage not to detach yourself emotionally in an attempt to avoid feeling their pain. You must be willing to bring your emotional sensitivity to bear and enter into their pain, and feel it yourself. If you are not willing to feel their pain, then, as they communicate to you about their challenges, their painful memories, and so forth, their situation can become a kind of detached problem, or abstract issue for you. You will tend to listen intellectually, trying to solve the problem as you would a mathematical equation, without truly understanding what they are feeling. Even when you try to be of service, you might make responses that are abstract and intellectual, that seem quite *logical* to you, but they cannot understand them, for they are overshadowed by the pain they are feeling, the confusion, the frustration. Your gift to them is to be as sensitive as possible, to truly *know* what it feels like to be in their position. You would do that, *to the best of your ability*.

Now, love is very large. Even if you are feeling their pain, you can continue to love them, and feel that they are a wonderful person. You feel the warmth and love toward them. And, it is very important that you *express* the warmth and love to them, for they will usually feel they are not lovable. They will feel that they are soiled, that they are not good enough to receive love. So, you will strive to feel their goodness, and to communicate it to them.

When you are trying to feel their goodness, it is not so beneficial to artificially pretend that you are feeling it, for they will usually sense the dishonesty. Therefore, this makes a demand upon you to truly open your heart to them. In spite of the difficulty of their challenge that you are feeling, you will need to strive to continue to see and feel their magnificence. This will require a great deal of openness on your part.

Another area that is important in helping your loved one is *discipline*. If you would say, "I have a difficult problem," and you try to solve it and you do not, you can become frustrated and simply ignore the problem. When you are listening to one who is asking you to help them heal the effects of child abuse, there will usually be much repetition of their thoughts, feelings, and memories that you have heard before. There can be a feeling in you that says, "This is too frightening. This is too challenging." At times, you might even feel, "This is too boring, too frustrating." It takes a certain amount of discipline to say, "No matter what I feel about this, I am dedicated to helping them with their healing. When they need me, I will give."

There are limits to your giving, of course. If one becomes *obsessed* with their healing process and they become overbalanced, then you can use your frustration response as a guide to communicate to them, ''Perhaps we have gone too far. Perhaps we need to make some release for a while.''

Many times, the loved one of an individual who struggles with the effects of child abuse can become caught up in a sense of *helplessness*. The loved one will try to help, but it seems to them that the abused one does not heal fast enough. If there is a loving, honest relationship between the loved one and the abused one, then there needs to be a certain kind of *exchange* between them. In other words, if you are the loved one, you could say to the abused one, ''I am committed to helping you heal, but, occasionally, I have my own frustrations, fears, and doubts. As part of our loving assistance to one another, occasionally, I will need for you to sit and listen to me, and love me, and help me vent these feelings that seem so troubling. Help me remember that they are *feelings*, not truths.''

So, if you, as the loved one who is trying to help, would feel, ''I am so frustrated with the challenge of my loved one, I cannot stand to go further, it is so hopeless and terrible,'' then say to yourself, ''These challenging feelings within me are important. I will not swallow them. I will try to have my beloved one help me with them, so that I can live through them and learn that they are simply feelings. It is not a truth that I am helpless to assist my loved one. It is true that I *feel* that I am helpless.'' The truth is that there is *always* reason for hope. *There is always the force of God to draw upon to heal anything, if you can believe in it.*

QUESTION: As an adult, is it important to the individual's healing process to *confront* the person who abused them when they were a child?

We would say quite strongly that *this must be an individual choice*. In some cases, there can be benefit for the one who was abused to confront the one who abused them. In others, a confrontation can unnecessarily exacerbate the challenges, the pain, and the suffering of all ones involved.

If you are one who has been abused, in order to make your own personal decision about whether or not to make a confrontation, you must do enough healing in the areas that we have pointed out so that you can come to a place where you feel your own sense of clarity about what is appropriate for your next step. If there is an extremely strong conviction in you that says, "I cannot be healed until I confront the one who abused me," then, most likely, you will need to confront. But, if you feel ambivalent—you have no strong feeling either way—then it is wise to wait until you *do* have a strong feeling one way or the other before you make your decision.

If you are growing in important areas of your life, and you are trusting yourself and your own feelings and thoughts, and you have a strong feeling that says, "It is best *not* to confront," then you must trust that feeling and follow it.

Again, this is an area where a decision must be made by the individual. It is wise to make certain that you do not feel that you *must* confront, simply because *others* feel that such confrontation is mandatory for healing. You are capable of healing in any way that you decide is appropriate for you.

QUESTION: Many people do not remember having been sexually abused as a child, and yet they have many fears in the sexual area. Sometimes therapists will suggest that they may have been abused as a child. How can a person determine if they have been sexually abused as a child when they have no conscious memory of such abuse?

First of all, we would point out to you ones of earth that you are extremely fond of *facts*. If you can *prove* that a thing actually happened, then you have a satisfying sense of "knowing the truth," because you are confident that "it really happened." Generally, this preoccupation with facts serves you well in your physical life on earth.

But, let us say that there is a female one of forty-five years of age who has a terrible fear of being touched sexually by male ones. And, she has no memory of being sexually abused as child. She comes forth with the feeling, "I cannot tolerate the touch of a male one sexually." Let us imagine that she begins to work with her fear in the present. She brings it to the surface of her awareness, and, with loving help from others, she speaks about how frightening it feels when a male one tries to touch her sexually. She realizes that her fear is only *feelings*, for, in most cases, there is nothing dangerous in the sexual touch of a male one, particularly if it is a loving relationship. Gradually, she comes to understand that there is fear in her in the *present*. As she gently works and heals the fear in the present. She becomes more trusting. Eventually, she is able to have a satisfying sexual union with a beloved male one. She is healed.

Now, in order to show you a way to grasp some difficult areas involved in determining if there has been childhood abuse or not, let us suggest that instead of the above scenario, this female one goes to a psychological therapist who would say, "I believe you have been sexually abused as a child." She would begin to ponder this with a great sense of dread. She would believe it to be true, and then she would feel, "How terrible it must have been when I was a child." Convinced by the therapist that "it actually happened," she feels compelled to discover the "facts." She struggles to recall memories of having been sexually abused as a child.

In her struggle to remember and heal herself, perhaps she unconsciously *manufactures* memories of having been abused, when, indeed, she was not. She unconsciously creates false memories of being sexually abused by her father. So, she would say, "Now I know what happened." She believes that she knows a *fact*. She believes, "My father came forth in my childhood and used me sexually, and frightened me. It is his touch I am afraid of." In this particular situation, she has created a false belief that the challenge now lives in the *past* with her father. And, let us say the father is dead. Then she would say, "The fact is, my father *caused* my fear. The fact is, he is dead, so he cannot heal my fear. The fact is, I am now trapped in my fear of being touched sexually."

This example shows you that having "factual" knowledge about the past is not always beneficial for healing in the present. Even if the female one *had* been abused by the father, searching through the past for facts could not heal her. She would still need to work with her fears and painful feelings in the *present*.

Let us gently suggest that, if you have fears in the sexual area, and you are working with your fears—bringing them to the surface, living through them, sharing them—and, as part of your work, if you have memories that seem to be of sexual abuse of you as a child, gently say to yourself, "I will bring these memories to the surface and decide if they are fact, or imagination." Perhaps you will never know with certainty. But, you can say, "It does not matter so much about the past, because the healing of my fear takes place in the present. It is in the present that I am frightened. It is not so important *why* I am frightened, although it helps my understanding a bit. What is important is whether I am willing to heal by bringing all of my fears and pain to the surface in the present."

If you have some memories of being abused in the past, be gentle with them, work honestly with them, do not hide them. If you have *no* memories, and you feel that you are healing well in the present, then you do not need memories of the past in order to heal. It is not so important what the "facts" of the past are. The past is ended.

We could assure you that most presently living human beings, *before* this present lifetime, at one point or another in the past, have been sexually molested as a child. So, if you root about enough within your consciousness, eventually, you might find a memory of being sexually abused as a child. Again, the "facts" are in the past. In this case, in a quite distant past. Your healing will be done in the present.

You are the one who must decide how important memories of past abuse are, and how important it is to seek out those memories. If you do decide to seek out memories of having been abused in the past, try not to *blame* the events of the past. Simply heal your painful memories, thoughts, and feelings in the present.

If you do not have memories of past sexual abuse, but you have challenges in the sexual area in the present, say to yourself, "I have enough to heal in the present. If memories wish to come, I invite them. If not, I will assume that I have none that are of great importance to my present challenge." If you have the courage, you can assume the *positive*. Most of you are quite willing to assume the *negative*.

QUESTION: Some people develop multiple personality disorders that seem to be the result of childhood abuse, particularly when there is very severe abuse. What causes this response, and how can it be healed?

As you could sense, the horribleness of certain abuse can seem overwhelming to a child. Some experiences can feel so terrible to the child that the personality of the child will desperately seek a way to *eliminate* the experience, eliminate the memories, eliminate the pain. And, when there is a feeling of hopelessness about any other way to heal, when there is not a loved one to turn to for help, when there is a feeling of total isolation and helplessness, often the structures within the mind that you would call the subconscious thought patterns, are called upon in a way to manufacture imaginary experiences to replace the horrible real ones that are taking place. This desperate manufacturing can touch into areas of fantasy that are based upon what a child has seen in this lifetime, stories that have been told, or various experiences of others that have been observed by the child. These fantasies can be taken up as an ''identity'' by being built upon and unconsciously created as an alternative life to the one that is so painful.

All of this is done almost automatically by powerful, imaginative capacities, thoughts, and emotional patterns that are, in a sense, out of control. The new, imaginary reality is desperately grabbed on to as a substitute for the horribly painful thoughts and feelings of the ordinary experience.

Some individuals, under the stress of childhood abuse, have a capacity to literally project themselves from their present personality into a personality that is unconsciously held in their memory from a past lifetime. In a sense, they can become who they were before this lifetime. This can happen as the person frantically searches for a life to lead that is not as frightening or as painful as their present life.

A rarer occurrence is when a person who has suffered abuse begins to frantically search for relief, and they draw upon their inner *psychic* abilities to sense the life of a presently living human being, and to intuit how that person thinks and feels. They will usually, unconsciously, choose to attune to a person who is joyful and confident. In a way, not always with total accuracy, but often with startling results, they will imaginatively live the life of a presently living human being.

All of this, you might say, is a function of the "animal" mind—the physical brain. The physical brain is rooted in the simple animal response of attraction to pleasure, and repulsion from pain.

Although the physical brain is controlled to some extent by the soul, and by the human mind structure that is *not* physical, the brain is still a manifestation of the physical, animal, human body. The animal brain, which directs the functions of the physical body, is "shared" by the soul, and by the personality of the human being. Human beings have the right and the freedom to override the harmonious, creative animal brain of their physical body. And, often, under the impact of terror, the harmonious animal nature can be seized upon by the frightened personality in the body, and the person can unconsciously *force* the physical brain into abnormal responses. In such a case, the person is desperately using the physical brain as a "mind," in an attempt to find a new life that is not so terrifying. This temporarily overrides the wiser, non-physical mind that ordinarily directs the physical brain. Thus, instead of a response directed by the non-physical mind, which is rooted in the wisdom of their larger being, they are making a response directed by the brain, which is rooted in the limited animal nature of the physical body. This is a very crude way to put it, but, at present, there are no human words for these complex inner functionings of the physical brain and the non-physical mind.

QUESTION: In the case of multiple personality disorders, what is required to integrate the person into one personality?

For some human beings, the personality will not be integrated in this lifetime. In a way, the "animal" decision to escape the present life is relatively irrevocable. The individual will simply live their life flitting about between what you might call "personalities," but which, in truth, are simply *sets of imaginings and mental structures*.

In general, the most powerful healing comes when the individual can make their "ordinary" personality more *habitable*. This means that they learn that the fear that they experience within themselves cannot destroy them. They learn that they are *creating* the terror that they feel, and they come to know that they can live through it and heal it. They learn that their personality is capable of creating experiences of love, safety, goodness, joy, and happiness. So, anything that leads in such a direction is usually helpful in the healing process.

It is also important that the ones helping the confused individual try to share warmth, understanding, and love. This will entice the "real" personality—the one *intended* for this lifetime—to participate with those who are helping make the life of the individual joyful, safe, and interesting. By sensitivity, warmth, and love, you encourage the terrified child that is hiding behind the other personality imaginings to feel that it is safe to come forth into the present moment. This is difficult, for the child within is terrified that the present is where pain and suffering live.

This gives you a *general* approach to these kinds of healings. Again, each individual case needs to be understood for its own unique qualities.

QUESTION: You have said in other teachings that each person's soul chooses their parents and their childhood environments. What are the reasons, from the soul's perspective, for a person to choose such a painful and traumatic experience as being abused when they are a child?

This is a very difficult area for you ones to understand, for you have created within yourselves such a fear of pain that you have made suffering and pain seem *horrible* and *terrible*. With such an attitude toward pain, it is almost impossible for some human beings to understand why a soul would choose to project a child into a family that most certainly will inflict pain upon the child.

So, for those who would be convinced that pain is horrible and terrible, we can not be of much service. We can only suggest that you gently work each day to try to realize that pain is *temporary*. Pain cannot destroy you. You have the forces of God itself to draw upon to heal pain. And, if you are courageous and confident enough, eventually you will heal all pain. Not because you are terrified of it and wish to eliminate it, but because you finally realize that it cannot damage you—your true being.

For those who are more willing to believe that pain is not horrible—although it is certainly not *desirable* to you— we would need to describe in the following manner the way that a soul might choose an abusive family. Imagine that you are an eternal soul, standing *before* your present physical birth. You have the capacity to look about at *all* living human beings. As you prepare to project a portion of yourself as a new human being into physical form, you have the freedom, in coordination with other souls, to choose *any father and mother on the face of the earth.*

As you prepare to make this soul choice, there are many patterns and energies that will generally turn your attention in certain directions—toward certain countries, a certain race, a certain social structure, and so forth. But, you are free to choose what pleases you. And, you have the vision to know what is most beneficial for the new child that you will project into earth. So, you must assume that the choice of your human family is a choice that is made in vast wisdom, understanding, and love.

Imagine that you as a soul are now making the choice of your family. You look about earth and you see a potential father and mother who are presently alive in human form, and, in past lifetimes of earth, have been deeply loved by you. Perhaps they were your own children in a past lifetime. And, let us say that you see them presently struggling in a large city of the United States. Perhaps, Baltimore. They are of a racial grouping that is being mistreated and intimidated, one that has had great pain and suffering, in general. In this lifetime, the male one is an alcoholic, and has uncontrolled sexual desires. The female is simple, perhaps not so intelligent, and she is constantly being beaten by the male one.

Now, you as a soul, looking at these two who were so beloved to you in past lifetimes, can see these patterns of challenge that they are presently manifesting. But, you are not frightened by them. You understand that the negative patterns are *temporary*. You even realize that if these two do not heal their negative patterns in their present lifetime, they will not be damaged in their being. You are fully aware that one human life is an instant in eternity, and, in so many lifetimes, these ones were your beloved ones. So, without the distortion of the human fear of pain and negativity, you truly love this male one and this female one, and you deeply understand their fear, their pain, and their suffering.

Thus, you as a soul would say, in effect, "I have been so deeply loved in the past by these two, particularly by this male one, that if I go forth to these two as a female child, then perhaps the male one might be touched so deeply in his heart with love for me that he might heal his present fears that cause such pain and turmoil in his life." You would know full well that if he does *not* heal, then your childhood will be extremely painful. But, you understand clearly that you have had even more painful human childhoods in past lifetimes, and none of them have damaged your being. But, to address the pain that you see that you might suffer as a female child in this family, you bring forth an "extra amount" of courage and strength to weave into your new female personality. You bring various capacities and abilities to heal yourself, if there is abuse of you by the fathering one. You bring forth determination, stamina, and persistence so that you can succeed in your life, even if your childhood is quite negative.

Then, when you are born as a human female child, each

one in the family begins to determine which patterns will affect you as they make their personal choices. Let us say that the father is *not* touched by you deeply enough to heal his fears. He continues his alcoholism and his uncontrolled sexual desire. You are sexually abused by the father. As a result, as you grow, you fall into your fears, your pain, your suffering, and you forget the great healing capacities that you as a soul placed into your personality. You do not use them. Instead, you curse your father and hate him. Your life is painful and terrible, from your point of view. Then, you die, seeing only *badness* in your father and your life, because it was *painful*. This does not change the fact that the *intention* of your soul in choosing your family was rooted in *goodness* and *love*. And, even the pain and suffering of your life does not diminish the love that still joins you to the father that abused you.

At this point in time, there is not enough depth to human words to bring satisfactory understanding of the soul's choice of a challenging family. But, this example may help you feel the *love* that would lead a soul to make such a choice.

QUESTION: Would you give us an inner process that can be used to further the healing of the effects of child abuse, and to promote self love?

We would say to you ones who carry the pain of childhood with you, to those who are troubled, confused, frightened, frustrated, and doubtful about yourself and your life, that no matter how bad you may feel in any moment, in truth, *you are deeply understood, and you are loved. You are not alone in your present experience of human life.*

For most of you, there are human beings who love you and understand you. For *all* of you, *there are eternal souls who stand beyond your earth perceptions, but who constantly pour forth their love into your heart as extraordinary energies and forces* that often you are not aware of.

There are beloved souls who inwardly share your pain and suffering with you, striving to help you feel the presence of love and goodness inside you.

Most important of all, *there is God itself, pouring forth unending energies and forces of love into you.* At times, in the struggles of earth life, it is difficult for you to feel this love, or even to believe that it exists. But, it is not so difficult to at least *say to yourself* each day:

"The forces of God love me. The forces of God sustain me. If I fall into despair and feel that I am abandoned by God, I must remind myself that this is a *feeling*, not a *truth*."

So, for this moment, and in those moments in each day in which you feel that you are lost in your human challenges, let yourself make a gentle relaxation within yourself, releasing all tension, worry, doubt, and fear. Acknowledge gently that at times you do have certain human feelings that seem quite terrible to you. At times, you have memories from the past that are very painful. You might even have periods of great suffering, horrible thoughts, and dark feelings. But, in this moment, gently remind yourself:

"All of my negative human experiences are *temporary*. The energies of love that constantly pour forth into me are *permanent*. This love will continue to fill me throughout this lifetime. It will continue to sustain me after the death of my present physical body."

Your challenge, of course, is that you have not *fully* learned to feel this force of love, and have not gained a trust in its permanence, because you have been *busy*, trying to fulfill in human life, and trying to heal the painful thoughts and feelings within your personality. So, say to yourself:

"In this moment, I do not wish to be busy. There is time in the future for fulfilling, and for healing challenges. In this moment, as a gift to myself, I wish to feel the *truth* of life. And, in this moment, the truth is, *there are extraordinary energies of love pouring into my being, from souls that love me and rejoice in me. From God itself. The truth is, this will never cease.*"

For this moment, as best you can, make a gentle softness in your heart. Let the old challenges slip away for a moment, and say to yourself:

"Whether I can feel it or not, in this moment, I am willing to imagine the extraordinary forces of love that are penetrating me. The hurt child within my personality is now coming forth to receive this love. To bask in it. To be healed by it."

The healing takes place as you open your heart, and as you allow yourself to be penetrated by a love that never ceases. In this moment, feeling the love, rejoicing in it, open your heart, and be healed.

Appendix

Appendix

Further Study with

Dr. Ron Scolastico

Ron Scolastico has brought wisdom and inspiration to individuals and groups throughout the world. His work has helped thousands of people to understand their human life as a magnificent expression of their eternal soul, and a manifestation of the forces of God.

Through his books and audio tapes, Dr. Scolastico has created a vast body of spiritual and psychological knowledge that provides brilliant insights into many areas of life. If you desire to study more of this material, you can request a free catalog of books and audio tapes by writing or telephoning:

Transpersonal Consultation Group
P.O. Box 6556
Woodland Hills, CA 91365
818-224-4488

ABOUT DR. RON SCOLASTICO

In 1978, Dr. Ron Scolastico began a journey that has led to his present work with the larger realities of life. As the result of a long series of extraordinary experiences spanning a period of several years, he became, as he describes it, "not the sedate university professor that I might have been," but a unique teacher and spiritual counselor who is able to enter a profound state of consciousness to draw upon an apparently unlimited source of spiritual wisdom and inspiration. Instead of teaching in the college classroom, he is now giving lectures, workshops, and individual *life readings* for thousands of people throughout the world.

Dr. Scolastico's personal experience with larger realities began in 1978. At that time, he was preparing to embark on a career as a university professor. While he was completing his doctorate degree at a major Midwestern university, he experienced some deep inner transformations that led him to question his goal of becoming a professor. After receiving his Ph.D. degree, he decided that instead of teaching Psychology and Human Communications in the college classroom, he would become a teacher of Spiritual Development.

Shortly after this decision, Dr. Scolastico's transformation was accelerated by a "reading" given to him by a spiritual teacher. Through this source, he was told that he had the ability to enter into a deep state of consciousness to tap a vast source of spiritual wisdom. At first, he doubted that he had the psychic ability described by the spiritual teacher. He says, "Even though I was quite knowledgeable in the area of human consciousness, having studied for many years everything I could find on the subject—from ancient mystical teachings, through humanistic and transpersonal psychology—and even though I had practiced meditation for more than ten years, I was not at all interested in 'psychic' explorations.'' He adds that, ''I believed that I knew myself quite well, and I was sure that I had no abilities in the psychic area.''

Even though he doubted the information from the spiritual teacher, Dr. Scolastico decided, out of curiosity, that he would test himself. In describing this test, he says:

> ''I devised a simple plan to carry out after my meditation each day. I would have a tape recorder standing by, and, at the end of the meditation, I would turn on the tape recorder and try to talk from the deep meditation state. Afterwards, I could evaluate what was said to see if it expanded upon my own knowledge, or if it brought through something that I didn't consciously know.''

At first, the results of his experiment seemed to prove to Dr. Scolastico that his doubts were well founded. He felt that during these meditative speakings he was simply expressing his own personal ideas and beliefs. ''For more than a month, the results were the same . . . I would speak about general ideas that were mundane and obvious, with me feeling normal as I spoke. Exactly what I had anticipated.'' Yet, surprisingly, he continued his experiment. Evey day, after his meditation period, he would speak into the tape recorder. He was enjoying the feeling of peace that came when he did these speakings.

The first unusual event that Dr. Scolastico experienced with his speakings occurred about a month after the beginning of his test. He describes it in this way:

> "I sat down and did my meditation as usual. Then I reached over and turned on the recorder, said my affirmation, and settled down into the now familiar sense of deep relaxation that always came before I started speaking. When I felt ready, I opened my mouth and began to speak. What I then heard nearly shocked me out of my deep state of attunement. Instead of my normal voice, a thick Irish brogue had popped out of my mouth!
>
> I stopped speaking and sat there with my eyes closed, inwardly examining myself, trying to objectively figure out what was going on. I felt normal, except for my sense of deep relaxation. There certainly wasn't any feeling of guides or anyone else making my words sound like an Irish brogue. Clearly, there wasn't anyone there but me. But I wasn't causing the Irish accent."

Along with the Irish accent, there came a deeper feeling of peace. Dr. Scolastico decided that somehow his unconscious mind was causing the accent. He decided to accept the accent and enjoy the satisfying feeling that came along with it.

His next experience of note worthiness occurred several weeks later when he decided to suggest to himself that his daily speaking would deal with a friend of his who was struggling emotionally. Dr. Scolastico says, "When the Irish voice came through, it immediately began to talk about Martha, discussing the causes of her turmoil and offering suggestions about ways she could change the situation.'' He felt that the advice given was the same advice that he would have given in his normal conscious state, so he concluded that the information was simply coming from his own mind.

Coincidently, the next day, his friend, Martha, happened to stop by Dr. Scolastico's house to see him. He explained his experiment to her and gave her the tape that he had done for her. The following day she called him. She was very excited. She told him that the tape was the most amazing thing she had ever heard in her life, and that it had helped her resolve her turmoil.

Gradually, Dr. Scolastico's friends heard about Martha's tape and asked him to do a ''reading'' for them. Explaining carefully that he believed the information came from his own mind, he agreed to their requests. Sitting alone in his meditative state, he would speak into the tape recorder about an individual, then he would give the person the tape. He says that the tapes ''seemed to be helpful, and the speakings were always positive, reassuring, and loving. Still, I was cautious about the process.''

Finally, after several months of doing these tapes in private, a friend, Lina, persuaded him to do a ''live'' reading for her. During this reading, Dr. Scolastico had a most profound experience that opened the door to his present work. He describes it in this way:

> ''I began to notice a strange sensation spreading through my body. It was as if the normal feeling of my body's weight was beginning to *dissolve*. Sud-

denly I began to feel very light, as if I had no weight. I was feeling like my body was made of air instead of flesh.

Then, an extremely intense feeling of *expansion* began to happen *by itself* within me. I had nothing to do with it. I was not creating the feeling. *It was being done to me by something other than myself.* I was gradually being expanded outward, growing larger. What I ordinarily experience as my conscious self, confined within the limits of my physical body, was now becoming a huge sphere of intense awareness that was beginning to fill the room. It was amazing. *I was soon clearly experiencing myself as actually filling the entire space of that room.* In addition, this expanded feeling brought with it an incredible feeling of love that was more profound than anything I had ever experienced.''

The experience in that moment was similar to something that had happened when Dr. Scolastico was eight years old. At that time, as a child, he had also expanded beyond his own conscious limits, but since the experience had frightened him, he had blocked it from his mind. Now, as his extraordinary experience within the reading continued, he says, "I felt a surge of energy flow through me, and instantly the Irish voice was speaking again.'' When the voice began to speak, it felt quite different than his previous experiments. "For the first time since I had begun practicing the speaking, it felt as if I had nothing to do with what was being said. The words did not feel as if they were originating within me. They were somehow being spoken *through* me, without me having any part in choosing the words or in speaking them."

The Irish voice began to explain to Lina that Dr. Scolastico had left his physical body. The voice told her that he was experiencing an expanded state of consciousness that was necessary in order to go beyond physical reality and attune to the source of knowledge upon which he was drawing. Then, as Dr. Scolastico describes it:

"Even though I had no idea where my body was or what was happening to it, I heard the voice say something that made me feel like the hairs on my head were standing up. The voice said: '*The experience of expansion that Ron is now having was first implanted in him when he was eight years old so that it could be returned at this time, so that he would believe.'* "

After this experience, Dr. Scolastico began to overcome his doubts. He began to do face to face personal readings for individuals on a regular basis. As word of his work spread, he was soon traveling throughout the United States, doing deep attunement sessions for individuals, and conducting seminars and workshops. Since 1978, Dr. Scolastico has done personal readings for more than 14,000 people around the world.

Dr. Scolastico feels that the primary message of his work with vast spiritual realities is that, "We *can* fully and completely manifest the magnificence of our soul in the everyday reality of our lives."

OTHER BOOKS BY DR. RON SCOLASTICO

HEALING THE HEART, HEALING THE BODY:
A Spiritual Perspective on Emotional, Mental, and Physical Health

The inspiring wisdom in this book was drawn from the vast source of spiritual knowledge to which Dr. Scolastico attunes. This is a comprehensive guide to health, healing, and spiritual realities. It offers a profound view of the relationship between the human personality, the physical body, and the soul.

In Dr. Scolastico's preface to *Healing the Heart, Healing the Body*, he addresses the fact that in our efforts to heal disease, "no single approach has been demonstrated to be consistently effective in healing *all* people at *all* times." He believes that the reason that we do not have a universally effective healing method is that, "even though our *physical bodies* might be relatively similar, there are complex *psychological* and *spiritual* factors that make each individual's healing a unique circumstance."

Dr. Scolastico points out that we may understand something about our physical bodies and our psychological patterns, yet, "many of us lack a clear understanding of how the nonphysical, *spiritual energies* in life can affect our health." He reminds us that spiritual energies continually interact with our bodies, our thoughts, and our emotions, but, "such energies are difficult for us to understand because they are usually hidden from our ordinary awareness." Dr. Scolastico says that *Healing the Heart, Healing the Body* in intended "to help bring the hidden spiritual energies into a clearer focus so that we may consciously draw upon them to create emotional, mental, and physical health in our lives.''

In **Chapter 1** of *Healing the Heart, Healing the Body*, Dr. Scolastico's inspired wisdom addresses our health and its relationship to the vast eternal forces of life. **Chapter 2** examines the important relationship between our human personality and our own soul. In **Chapter 3**, there is beneficial knowledge about the cause of human illness. **Chapter 4** gives us an in-depth look at the way that the choices and energies of our soul will affect our physical health. In **Chapter 5**, there is knowledge that will help us learn to observe our inner patterns of thinking and feeling so that we may identify the ones that can block our health. The important area of our human desires is examined in **Chapter 7,** and we are shown how the loving understanding of desires can be a part of creating health. **Chapter 8** brings us fascinating and beneficial new insights into the power of the mind, and shows the dramatic impact our thoughts can have upon our physical health. **Chapter 9** takes us into the powerful, and at times confusing world of our emotions. We are shown the important part that our feelings play in the manifestation of either health, or illness. In **Chapter 10**, we are shown how we can use the power of our beliefs about life to create the strong inner forces that can help us live a healthy life. **Chapter 11** shows us how the use of our will in choosing day by day can either block health-giving energies, or intensify them. In **Chapter 12**, the various aspects of our inner lives are brought together in a deep understanding of our whole personality experience. We are shown how to work with our personality in ways that can create health and joy. **Chapter 13** examines the relationship between our inner life and the physical reality of the outer world, showing us how important our inner life is in determining what we manifest in the physical world. **Chapter 14** offers a profound method for bringing together all of our knowledge about our inner life and the outer world in order to create health and healing for our physical bodies. In **Chapter 15**, Dr. Scolastico's inspired wisdom gives us ways to work day by day to in our inner life, and in the outer world, to create a healthy life, mentally, emotionally, and physically.

Healing the Heart, Healing the Body is a profoundly helpful "user's guide" for the human mind, emotions, and body. It is one of those rare books that can help you tap into your inner wisdom in a way that can make your journey through life more healthful, more loving, and more fulfilling.

Marianne Williamson, author of *A Return to Love* says, "Ron Scolastico is an important guide to higher wisdom. *Healing the Heart, Healing the Body* is a marvelous contribution to anyone interested in the connection between spirituality and healing."

Psychiatrist, Dr. Harold Bloomfield, author of *Making Peace With Your Parents*, believes that Dr. Scolastico's book, *Healing the Heart, Healing the Body,* "is a must read book for anyone wanting greater health. It is also a must read book for anyone on the spiritual path. It is a must read book for everyone."

THE EARTH ADVENTURE:
Your Soul's Journey Through Physical Reality

The Earth Adventure is Dr. Scolastico's first book of wisdom drawn from a vast source spiritual knowledge. It will take you on a journey with your soul through the universe—from its beginnings, to the present, and into the future.

In the Introduction to *The Earth Adventure*, Dr. Scolastico writes about how he discovered his ability to tap into spiritual knowledge that exists beyond ordinary consciousness. He shares the moving, and sometimes baffling experiences that led to his unfoldment as a spiritual teacher.

In **Chapter 1**, the inspired wisdom looks at who we are as human beings, describes our origin as souls, and gives us suggestions for opening to a direct perception of the beginning of life. **Chapter 2** focuses upon the creation of the physical reality of earth. It explains in detail how we, as souls, participated in the process of bringing the physical world into existence. In **Chapter 3**, we are shown how human beings extended the forces of the souls in ancient periods in order to create early civilizations. There is an enlightening look at how humans brought negativity into earth life. **Chapter 4** gives us an extraordinary look at the soul forces that are involved in the creation of living human beings, from the initial formation of personality energies, to the miraculous process of projecting those personality energies into a human body at birth. In **Chapter 5**, our life as a human being is examined in detail, with a look at the development of our

mental and emotional capacities, from a spiritual perspective. **Chapter 6** will give you a deep new understanding of your development as a human being, from childhood through your later years. **Chapter 7** examines the
mysteries of death, and shows us what we will experience
after the death of our physical body. In **Chapter 8**, you
will enter into the extraordinary world of your eternal
soul, and you will learn how your soul, after your death
in this lifetime, will create the new personality that will be
you in a future lifetime. **Chapter 9** will give you the
knowledge necessary to live a more fulfilling life, including an understanding of ways to work with your various
levels of consciousness.

The Earth Adventure will inspire you to bring forth the
deeper aspects of your being to create the joy and love
that you desire in your life. Dr. Barbara DeAngelis, Best-
Selling author and teacher says, ''I found *The Earth Adventure* to be a mystical and powerfully moving source of
wisdom and inspiration that helps teach all of us how to
master the relationship we have with our own spirit.''

You can obtain *The Earth Adventure*, and *Healing the
Heart, Healing the Body* at your local book store.

If you would like to receive a catalog of Hay House products, or information about future workshops, lectures, and events sponsored by the Louise L. Hay Educational Institute, please detach and mail this questionnaire.

We hope you receive value from *Reflections*. Please help us evaluate our distribution program by filling out this brief questionnaire. Upon receipt of this postcard, your catalog will be sent promptly.

NAME_____

ADDRESS_____

_____

I purchased this book from:

☐ Store_____

   City_____

☐ Other (Catalog, Lecture, Workshop)

   Specify_____

Occupation_____ Age_____

We hope you receive value from *Reflections*. Please help us evaluate our distribution program by filling out this brief questionnaire. Upon receipt of this postcard, your catalog will be sent promptly.

NAME_____

ADDRESS_____

_____

I purchased this book from:

☐ Store_____

   City_____

☐ Other (Catalog, Lecture, Workshop)

   Specify_____

Occupation_____ Age_____